BURTON COLLEGE LIBRARY
87210
WITHDRAWN

Collins
English for Exams

Reading
for IELTS

Els Van Geyte

Collins

HarperCollins Publishers Ltd
1 London Bridge Street
London
SE1 9GF

First edition 2011

10 9 8 7 6

© HarperCollins Publishers 2011

ISBN 978-0-00-742327-9

Collins ® is a registered trademark of HarperCollins Publishers Limited.

www.collinselt.com

A catalogue record for this book is available from the British Library.

Typeset in India by Aptara

Printed in China by RR Donnelley APS

All rights reserved. No part of this book may be reproduced, stored in a retrieval system, or transmitted in any form or by any means, electronic, mechanical, photocopying, recording or otherwise, without the prior permission in writing of the Publisher. This book is sold subject to the conditions that it shall not, by way of trade or otherwise, be lent, re-sold, hired out or otherwise circulated without the publisher's prior consent in any form of binding or cover other than that in which it is published and without a similar condition including this condition being imposed on the subsequent purchaser.

HarperCollins does not warrant that www.collinselt.com or any other website mentioned in this title will be provided uninterrupted, that any website will be error free, that defects will be corrected, or that the website or the server that makes it available are free of viruses or bugs. For full terms and conditions please refer to the site terms provided on the website.

About the author

Els Van Geyte has been teaching at the English for International Students Unit at the University of Birmingham (UK) for over 10 years, preparing her students for the IELTS exam and for the linguistic demands of their academic courses. Els is also the author of *Get Ready for IELTS Reading* (Collins, 2012).

Author's acknowledgements

I would like to mention Tasia Vassilatou, whose editorial skills and diplomatic feedback have been much appreciated. Thank you also to Howard Middle, who managed this project, to Celia and Catherine at HarperCollins, and to my first readers: Liz, Emma, John and Becky.

I would like to dedicate this book to John and Becky McCarthy, whose continual support has been invaluable.

HarperCollins would like to acknowledge the following contributors for material used in this publication courtesy of nisyndication.com:

From *The Times*: Spouses to receive more upon death of partner / Lauren Thompson; Still heading 'home' for Christmas? / Anna Shephard; Grandparents seek contact with grandchildren after family separation / Rosemary Bennett; Stress-free sleepovers / Sarah Ebner; Clueless parents fail the first aid test / Alexandra Frean; Increasing obesity pushes diabetes drug bill to £600m / Sam Lister; Rising school fees mean it's best to save now / Clare Francis; Education: Solving the special needs schools crisis / Zoe Brennan; Student anger and university delight greet unlimited fees / Greg Hurst and Joanna Sugden; Misery for parents as nursery fees are set to rise by 15% / Rosemary Bennett; It's the scary tea shop: one dunk and you're out / Alan Hamilton; Envirowise shows way to profit from environment care / Michelle Henery; Underwater archaeology: alien environment can sink the experts / Lewis Smith; Tow-surfing: why are the tides turning on us? / John-Paul Flintoff; Hot rocks harnessed in Cornwall / Ben Marlow; Poor NHS communication leaves elderly at risk of superbugs / David Rose; Body language speaks volumes / Carol Lewis; Monkey-friendly tunes shed new light on evolutionary role of music / Mark Henderson; Scot leads way in language at touch of a button / Kenny Kemp; Scientist discovers animal language / Jonathan Leake; Smarter than we think / Jonathan Leake and Georgia Warren; The kids' experiment / Sam Lister; Air travel hit as volcano hurls up new ash cloud / Jonathan Leake; Iceland's Eyjafjallajokull volcano roars back into life with new eruption / Hannah Devlin; A year abroad can make all the difference in job market / Joanna Sugden; Good University Guide 2010: Keep the faith – a degree is still a passport to better job prospects / Alexandra Frean; Jilted generation has all the icing – but no cake / Ben Machell; One in six young Britons jobless as unemployment hits 14-year high / Tom Bawden and Marcus Leroux; Why it's best to marry in your twenties / Andrew G. Marchall, Liam Plowman, Lucy MacDonald; Community spirit adds value to your home / Emma Wells; Prince of Wales backs Street Pride campaign to protect public spaces / Valerie Elliott; That's the community spirit / Lucy Denyer; You want my vote? Here's what I want in return / Siobhan Maguire; Will you love your neighbours? / Robert Bullard; Is high culture too pricey? Not at all / Richard Morrison; Cut-out-and keep guide to saving the arts / Bryan Appleyard; Why watching TV won't turn your baby into a genius / Helen Rumbelow; Is this a carbuncle I see before me? / Tom Dyckhoff; The different ways the world counts / Alex Bellos; Cyclists fuming over 'worse than useless bicycle lanes / Cian Ginty; Little and large a lethal combination: The growing popularity of "Chelsea tractors"? / Ben Webster; Briefing: Tourist tax / Colin Gleeson; Chinese come in search of history, culture and luxury shopping / Dominic Walsh; Tourists shun travel agents to book direct / Jeremy Skidmore; 'World's shortest flight' can ferry pupils to school in less than a minute / Melanie Reid; Pick up a Picasso for less than £1,000 / Mark Bridge; Mine rescue on verge of breakthrough / Martin Fletcher; Nicked by the mini robot in the sky / Emma Smith; Soaring CCTV cameras are 'costly, futile, and politically motivated' / Lindsay McIntosh

From *The Sunday Times*: Me Jane: Meet the real queen of the jungle / Jo Harvey; Scientists say dolphins should be treated as 'nonhuman persons' / Jonathan Leake; How to fast-track yourself into a job / David Malcolm

Photo credits

All images are from Shutterstock
Cover image © East/Shutterstock.com

MIX
Paper from
responsible sources
FSC™ C007454

FSC
www.fsc.org

FSC™ is a non-profit international organisation established to promote the responsible management of the world's forests. Products carrying the FSC label are independently certified to assure consumers that they come from forests that are managed to meet the social, economic and ecological needs of present and future generations, and other controlled sources.

Find out more about HarperCollins and the environment at
www.harpercollins.co.uk/green

Contents

Introduction

Who is this book for?

Reading for IELTS will prepare you for the IELTS Academic Reading test whether you are taking the test for the first time, or re-sitting the test. It has been written for learners with band score 5-5.5 who are trying to achieve band score 6 or higher.

The structured approach and comprehensive answer key have been designed so that you can use the materials to study on your own. However, the book can also be used as a supplementary reading skills course for IELTS preparation classes. The book provides enough material for approximately 50 hours of classroom activity.

Content

Reading for IELTS is divided into 12 units. Each unit focuses on a topic area that you are likely to meet in the IELTS exam. This helps you to build up a bank of vocabulary and ideas related to a variety of the topics. As in the IELTS test, the texts are taken from authentic sources. These may contain narratives, logical arguments, descriptions or discussions. Some of texts contain visuals.

Units 1–11 cover the types of question that you will see in the IELTS test. Each unit focuses on a particular type of question, for example, matching questions, short-answer questions, completion questions, multiple choice, questions asking you to identify information or identify writers' views or claims.

The exercises in the unit are relevant to the test. The aims listed at the start of each unit specify the key skills, techniques and language covered in the unit. You work towards Unit 12, which provides a final practice IELTS Reading test.

Additionally, the book provides examination strategies telling you what to expect and how best to succeed in the test. Exam information is presented in clear, easy-to-read chunks. 'Exam tips' in each unit highlight essential exam techniques and can be rapidly reviewed at a glance.

Unit structure

Each of the first 11 units is divided into 3 parts.

Part 1 introduces vocabulary related to the topic, often in the context of short texts. There are a range of exercises to help you to understand and use the vocabulary. The focus is on strategies and activities that are useful in the context of reading skills, for example working out the meaning of unknown words through the meaning of word components, or by examining word forms. The vocabulary is presented using Collins COBUILD dictionary definitions.

Part 2 provides information and practice on the task types you will come across in the IELTS Reading test. An explanation on each task type is followed by exercises of increasing difficulty. These exercises give you the opportunity to practise the skills that are needed to complete the task, and they help you to develop strategies for completing these tasks in the test. For example, in the unit about completing notes, and summaries, you develop strategies such as predicting what words may be missing by using your knowledge of grammar. You can then use this strategy when sitting the test.

Part 3 provides exam practice which focuses on the task that you practised in the unit. There is a text with questions. The number of questions is similar to the number in the actual test for the particular task type. You can use this as a way of assessing your readiness for the actual exam.

Answer key

A comprehensive answer key is provided for all sections of the book including suggested answers. Notes are also given on why certain answers are correct or incorrect.

Using the book for self-study

If you are new to IELTS, we recommend that you work systematically through the 12 units in order to benefit from its progressive structure. If you are a more experienced learner, you can use the aims listed at the start of each unit to select the most useful exercises.

Each unit contains between three and four hours of study material. Having access to someone who can provide informed feedback on reading practice exercises is an advantage. However, you can still learn a lot working alone or with a study partner willing to give and receive peer feedback.

Ideally, you should begin each unit by working through the **Part 1** vocabulary exercises. Try to answer the questions without looking at a dictionary in order to develop the skill of inferring the meaning of unfamiliar words from context. This is important because dictionaries cannot be used during the actual exam. Avoid writing the answers to vocabulary exercises directly into the book so that you can try the exercises again once you have completed the unit.

Take time to work through the **Part 2** exercises from beginning to end. It is important to study the notes about each of the task types so that you know the how to approach the different task types in the test. Doing this will also help you develop more general skills for reading. The strategies covered should be thoroughly mastered so that during the actual exam you are fully prepared for each section and can focus on reading and answering the questions. In the IELTS test itself, there is a time limit and you usually have to work fast, but while studying Part 2 of each unit in this book, take your time and learn as much as you can about the different task types.

Reading is a skill that can only be improved through extensive practice. The IELTS reading test can cover almost any topic considered to be within the grasp of a well-educated person. Therefore, you should aim to become well-informed about a wide variety of subjects, not just those covered in the book. Regularly reading English language materials on subjects such as science, business and education, can help with this, too.

In **Part 3** you are given the opportunity to put the strategies that you have learnt in Part 2 into practice. Work through the exercises at a reasonable speed. Again, check the answers carefully and learn from the notes provided in the Answer key. Also, remember to read the question carefully and complete the task in the exact way you have been asked. Do not assume that you know a particular task because you have practised similar ones in the past. There may be slight variations in the tasks in the actual IELTS test.

Unit 12 is a complete practice reading test. This unit should be done under exam conditions. Remember that the total allocated time is 60 minutes; there is no extra time to transfer answers. Please bear this in mind when doing Unit 12.

The International English Language Testing System (IELTS) Test

IELTS is jointly managed by the British Council, Cambridge ESOL Examinations and IDP Education, Australia.

There are two versions of the test:

- Academic
- General Training

Academic is for students wishing to study at undergraduate or postgraduate levels in an English-medium environment.

General Training is for people who wish to migrate to an English-speaking country.

This book is primarily for students taking the Academic version.

The Test

There are four modules:

Listening	30 minutes, plus 10 minutes for transferring answers to the answer sheet NB: the audio is heard *only once*. Approx. 10 questions per section Section 1: two speakers discuss a social situation Section 2: one speaker talks about a non-academic topic Section 3: up to four speakers discuss an educational project Section 4: one speaker gives a talk of general academic interest
Reading	60 minutes 3 texts, taken from authentic sources, on general, academic topics. They may contain diagrams, charts, etc. 40 questions: may include multiple choice, sentence completion, completing a diagram, graph or chart, choosing headings, yes/no, true/false questions, classification and matching exercises.
Writing	Task 1: 20 minutes: description of a table, chart, graph or diagram (150 words minimum) Task 2: 40 minutes: an essay in response to an argument or problem (250 words minimum)
Speaking	11–14 minutes A three-part face-to-face oral interview with an examiner. The interview is recorded. Part 1: introductions and general questions (4–5 mins) Part 2: individual long turn (3–4 mins) – the candidate is given a task, has one minute to prepare, then talks for 1–2 minutes, with some questions from the examiner. Part 3: two-way discussion (4–5 mins): the examiner asks further questions on the topic from Part 2, and gives the candidate the opportunity to discuss more abstract issues or ideas.
Timetabling	Listening, Reading and Writing must be taken on the same day, and in the order listed above. Speaking can be taken up to 7 days before or after the other modules.
Scoring	Each section is given a band score. The average of the four scores produces the Overall Band Score. You do not pass or fail IELTS; you receive a score.

IELTS and the Common European Framework of Reference

The CEFR shows the level of the learner and is used for many English as a Foreign Language examinations. The table below shows the approximate CEFR level and the equivalent IELTS Overall Band Score:

CEFR description	CEFR code	IELTS Band Score
Proficient user	C2	9
(Advanced)	C1	7–8
Independent user	B2	5–6.5
(Intermediate – Upper Intermediate)	B1	4–5

This table contains the general descriptors for the band scores 1–9:

IELTS Band Scores		
9	Expert user	Has fully operational command of the language: appropriate, accurate and fluent with complete understanding.
8	Very good user	Has fully operational command of the language, with only occasional unsystematic inaccuracies and inappropriacies. Misunderstandings may occur in unfamiliar situations. Handles complex detailed argumentation well.
7	Good user	Has operational command of the language, though with occasional inaccuracies, inappropriacies and misunderstandings in some situations. Generally handles complex language well and understands detailed reasoning.
6	Competent user	Has generally effective command of the language despite some inaccuracies, inappropriacies and misunderstandings. Can use and understand fairly complex language, particularly in familiar situations.
5	Modest user	Has partial command of the language, coping with overall meaning in most situations, though is likely to make many mistakes. Should be able to handle basic communication in own field.
4	Limited user	Basic competence is limited to familiar situations. Has frequent problems in understanding and expression. Is not able to use complex language.
3	Extremely limited user	Conveys and understands only general meaning in very familiar situations. Frequent breakdowns in communication occur.
2	Intermittent user	No real communication is possible except for the most basic information using isolated words or short formulae in familiar situations and to meet immediate needs. Has great difficulty understanding spoken and written English.
1	Non user	Essentially has no ability to use the language beyond possibly a few isolated words.
0	Did not attempt the test	No assessable information provided.

Marking

The Listening and Reading papers have 40 items, each worth one mark if correctly answered. Here are some examples of how marks are translated into band scores:

Listening: 16 out of 40 correct answers: band score 5
23 out of 40 correct answers: band score 6
30 out of 40 correct answers: band score 7

Reading 15 out of 40 correct answers: band score 5
23 out of 40 correct answers: band score 6
30 out of 40 correct answers: band score 7

Writing and Speaking are marked according to performance descriptors.
Writing: examiners award a band score for each of four areas with equal weighting:

- Task achievement (Task 1)
- Task response (Task 2)
- Coherence and cohesion
- Lexical resource and grammatical range and accuracy

Speaking: examiners award a band score for each of four areas with equal weighting:

- Fluency and coherence
- Lexical resource
- Grammatical range
- Accuracy and pronunciation

For full details of how the examination is scored and marked, go to: www.ielts.org

1 Family matters

Exam focus: Matching headings
Aims: Skim-reading | Understanding the structure of a paragraph
Understanding the function of a paragraph | Summarising paragraphs

Part 1: Vocabulary

1 What is the difference in meaning between the words in the groups 1–8? Use a dictionary to help you.

1	friend / mate / flatmate	**5**	colleague / business partner
2	sister / sister-in-law	**6**	acquaintance / stranger
3	brother / sister / sibling	**7**	aunt / great-aunt
4	boyfriend / husband / partner	**8**	half-sister / step-sister

2 Collocations are words that are often found together. Complete the sentences 1–4 with the words a–f. Note how they collocate with the words in italics.

a	abilities	**c**	apart	**e**	non-identical
b	adulthood	**d**	lifelong	**f**	older

1 Twins have a(n) _____ *bond* that other siblings may envy: they share their own language, play their own games from early childhood, share bedrooms and birthday parties.

2 James and his brother Frank are _____ *twins*, and they don't look alike at all.

3 A few years ago we sent out a questionnaire to pairs of twins asking about their *psychic* _____, and one identical twin in five reported some kind of telepathy.

4 Surprisingly, the 'twin effect' can become stronger as twins *grow* _____ and *move* _____. Often the older one will be dominant until they *reach* _____.

3 Underline the words related to the topic of family in the passage. Do not use a dictionary. Do Exercise 4 before you check your answers.

Widows and widowers whose spouses pass away without making a will are set to receive a bigger inheritance payout from next month. If a person dies without making a will, the amount left automatically to his or her spouse or civil partner is changing from £125,000 to £250,000 where there are children.

Experts have welcomed the change, which takes effect on February 1, but emphasise that it is still important to make a will, particularly if you are unmarried or separated but not divorced. However, people should not be misled into thinking that these changes mean that they do not need to make a will. It still remains the case that unmarried couples are not entitled to receive anything on the death of their other half if he or she has not made a will.

Modern family life is becoming ever more complicated, with second marriages and children from more than one relationship. A will is the only way to ensure that those you love or are obliged to care for are adequately provided for. After the spouse has received his or her legal share, the rest of the estate is shared by children or grandchildren. If there are none, surviving parents will get a share. If there are none of these, any brothers and sisters who shared the same two parents as the deceased will receive a share.

If your family circumstances have changed, it is important that you make or update a will to ensure that your money and possessions are distributed according to your wishes. For example, you may be separated and your ex-partner now lives with someone else. If you are married or enter into a registered civil partnership, this will invalidate any previous will you have made.

4 Match the words and phrases 1–12 from the passage in Exercise 3 with the definitions a–l. The words and phrases relating to the topic of death have been shaded.

1	widow	a	a husband or wife, considered in relation to their partner (formal)
2	widower	b	a former member of an established couple
3	spouse	c	to have stopped living together as a couple
4	will	d	somebody's wife, husband or partner
5	inheritance	e	a person who has recently died
6	ex-partner	f	a woman whose husband has died and who has not married again
7	(be) separated	g	money or property which you receive from somebody who has died
8	(be) divorced	h	a man whose wife has died and who has not married again
9	other half (informal)	i	a document in which a person declares what should be done with their money and property after they die
10	estate	j	to be legally separated from a husband or wife because the marriage has ended
11	deceased (*noun*)	k	to prove that an argument, conclusion, or result is wrong or cause it to be wrong
12	invalidate	l	all the money and property somebody leaves behind them when they die

Part 2: Practice exercises

 Exam information: Matching headings

This task tests whether you understand the organisation of texts and can identify the main idea or topic in each section of a text.

You will be given a numbered list with headings, as well as a text divided into sections. The headings will be in the form of short statements which summarise the information in a section. You will need to read the text sections and decide which of the headings best fits that section.

Exam tip: You have limited time to take the IELTS exam, so read only what you need to know in order to do the task. It is a good idea to read the first sentence of a short paragraph only. In longer paragraphs, read the first and last sentence. This technique is called 'skim-reading'.

1 Skim-read the text below. Then write one sentence saying what it is about. Do not look back at the text, but use your own words.

If you're in your thirties or forties and still going back to the family home for every big family celebration, any problems that have developed with your parents over the years are likely to be mentioned. You can easily end up remembering childhood problems and start behaving like an angry child, but you should try to resist this. Parents, meanwhile, should remember that they are no longer in charge of their children's lives. Parents need to enjoy their children for who they are now, as adults, rather than behaving like they did when they had more control over them.

2 The content of a paragraph is linked to its structure. The questions 1–9 will help you to understand the content and structure of the paragraphs a–c.

Paragraph a
Almost half of all grandparents lose all contact with their grandchildren after a separation or divorce, according to a new report. It found that forty-two per cent never see their grandchildren again after the break-up. Even more – sixty-seven per cent – are prevented from providing any sort of childcare or taking their grandchildren on outings, even when they had done so regularly in the past.

1 Which sentence is the topic sentence, the one that summarises the main idea(s) in the paragraph?

2 Does the paragraph as a whole become more specific or more general?

3 The second sentence mentions 'the break-up'. What does this refer to, and why is 'the' used, and not 'a'?

Paragraph b
The value of grandparents to children should not be underestimated. The report shows the need for the government to address the importance of grandparents in future policy and legislation. It also demonstrates the need to amend the Children Act 1989 to remove the obstacle that requires the biological family to ask permission prior to making an application to the court for contact. Especially when a family is going through difficulties, it is important that the children can turn to someone who is not directly involved and is calm and relaxed, and that person is often a grandparent.

4   The paragraph says 'The value of grandparents to children should not be underestimated'. Is this the same as saying that the value of grandparents to children is very important?

5   Which sentence expresses a similar idea to the first sentence, but with more detail?

6   Which sentence is the topic sentence?

Paragraph c
To have a society that is family-friendly, anti-discrimination laws will need to be introduced. Parenting would become a school subject, staircases would be rebuilt so that buggies and prams could access any building and advertising for sweets and non-educational toys would be forbidden. Companies would be forced to only employ people who can travel to work in less than forty minutes and there would also be a thirty-five-hour working week and more holidays. In a world like this, there would be less divorce and crime, but we would be earning and producing less.

7   Identify the introduction, the main body, and the conclusion of this paragraph.

8   Which of these three parts gives you the most important information?

9   The first sentence mentions a society that is 'family-friendly'. You may know words like 'environmentally friendly', 'child-friendly' and 'eco-friendly'. What does 'friendly' mean in this context?

3   **Which paragraph a–c in Exercise 2 ...**

1   states cause and effect? _____

2   develops an argument? _____

3   gives information/a description? _____

4   Write short headings for the passages 1–3.

1 _____

Nicholson defines the traditional family as 'the unit of parents with children who live together'. The bond between husband and wife is seen as particularly important, and the family feels itself to be separate from other kin. This family group is often referred to as the nuclear family.

2 _____

Traditional families have disadvantages:

- Because both partners now tend to work, they have tremendous time pressures, making it difficult to carry out satisfactory and rewarding childcare.
- Children who are the victims of abuse by parents have relatively little opportunity to turn to other relatives for help.
- Traditional families place a heavy burden of expectation on the partners, and, with work and childcare commitments, it may be difficult for them to provide the love and companionship each partner expects.

However, traditional families do have some advantages:

- Their small size tends to encourage intimacy between family members, and, when the relationships work, they can be rewarding and long-lasting.
- Traditional families can be economically successful because they are not usually expected to share their resources with others.

3 _____

Having someone else's child stay overnight is quite a responsibility. Some children begin having sleepovers with friends during the early school years, others still haven't started by age 11. It is important not to start too early: just because they say they want to have a sleepover at someone else's house, doesn't mean it's a good idea. When there is a sleepover at your house, be prepared with some strategies to get the children to stop talking and calm down. Agree lights out time in advance and have some calmer activities before bedtime.

5   The following passage has five sections, a–e. Choose the correct heading for sections a–e from the list of numbered headings i–ix. Follow these steps; they will help you do the exercise.

- In this task, there are more headings than sections, so read the sections first. (If there were the same number of sections as headings, it would be a good idea to read the headings first.)
- For each section of the passage, read the beginning and the end. Some of the sentences are long so there is no need to read the whole sentence. Underline some key words.
- Read the headings next. If they are long, underline some key words.
- You may now already be able to match some of the headings to the sections.
- Look at the remaining sections in more detail to help you match them to the headings.

List of headings

i New families: beneficial or harmful?	vi Families: then and now
ii The government reaction	vii The first criticisms of 'family'
iii The typical western family	viii The 'happy family' model
iv Political families	ix The function of families
v The disappearance of the traditional model	

Section a

The family has often been regarded as the cornerstone of society. In premodern and modern societies alike it has been seen as the most basic unit of social organization and one which carries out vital tasks, such as socializing children.

Section b

Until the 1960s few sociologists questioned the importance or the benefits of family life. Most sociologists assumed that family life was evolving as modernity progressed, and that the changes involved made the family better suited to meeting the needs of society and of family members. A particular type of family, the nuclear family (based around a two-generation household of parents and their children), was seen as well adapted to the demands of modern societies.

Section c

From the 1960s, an increasing number of critical thinkers began to question the assumption that the family was necessarily a beneficial institution. Feminists, Marxists and critical psychologists began to highlight what they saw as some of the negative effects and the 'dark side' of family life.

In the following decades the family was not just under attack from academic writers. Social changes also seemed to be undermining traditional families. Rising divorce rates, cohabitation before marriage, increasing numbers of single-parent families and single-person households, and other trends all suggested that individuals were basing their lives less and less around conventional families.

Section d

Some have seen these changes as a symptom of greater individualism within modern societies. They have welcomed what appears to be an increasing range of choice for individuals. People no longer have to base their lives around what may be outmoded and, for many, unsuitable conventional family structures. Others, however, have complained about the changes and worried about their effect on society. Such changes are seen as both a symptom and a cause of instability and insecurity in people's lives and in society as a whole. This view has been held by traditionalists who want a return to the ideal of the nuclear family. For them, many of society's problems are a result of increased family instability.

Section e

Alongside these developments in society and sociology, family life has become a topic of political debate. Politicians have become somewhat more willing to comment on families. Sometimes they have devised policies to try to deal with perceived problems surrounding the family. In short, the family has come to be seen as more problematic than it was in the past. The controversies that have come to surround families and households are the subject of this chapter.

Section a	_____		Section d	_____
Section b	_____		Section e	_____
Section c	_____			

READING PASSAGE

*This reading passage has 5 sections, **A–E**.*

Choose the correct heading for sections A–E from the list of numbered headings below. Write the correct number i–viii next to sections A–E.

List of Headings

i	The science of marriage
ii	The importance of honest communication
iii	The power of thought
iv	The likelihood of marrying again
v	Technological advances
vi	The benefits of avoiding arguments
vii	The real predictor for a lasting marriage
viii	The consequences of early dissatisfaction

Section A   _____

Section B   _____

Section C   _____

Section D   _____

Section E   _____

Section A

Marriage is a much-researched topic, and the way married couples communicate in particular has been the subject of many studies. These days, research into marriage often involves hours of recordings, followed by a thorough analysis of data with the help of modern software applications.

Section B

One such study analysed five years' worth of data, obtained from 750 participating couples. At the start of the study, participants who felt they were in a harmonious relationship reported having happy marriages. In other words, low levels of conflict corresponded to a perceived higher degree of happiness. At the end of the five-year period, however, many of these couples had separated or had started divorce proceedings. The outcome of this study suggests that keeping the peace rather than talking about problems and working through them can have harmful effects on a relationship.

Section C

In a more recent, larger scale study, people were observed over a fifteen-year period. The researchers recorded the timings of marriages, divorces and remarriages and discovered patterns that helped them estimate how likely divorce was. If participants admitted the possibility of divorce to themselves during the first year of the study, the probability of it actually happening was ten times greater than for those couples who had not thought about it at all. Clearly, once the idea of divorce is in somebody's mind, they are more likely to act on it.

Section D

Yet another piece of research confirms that the way men and women feel at the beginning of their marriage makes a difference to its eventual outcome. Those who feel disappointed, perhaps because marriage itself is different from their expectations, or because their lifestyle is not what they had envisaged, are more likely to divorce.

Section E

Having said that, relationships are complex and their development is the result of many different influences. The end of a marriage is unlikely to be brought about by one particular factor, and is more probably the result of a combination of small incidents that add up over time. It is also worth bearing in mind that in most countries it is the minority of marriages that fail. No one can truthfully claim that their marriage is happy or perfect all the time, but the fact remains that most married people stay together for life. The secret of a happy marriage, it seems, lies where most people have always thought it does: in the effort made on a daily basis by both partners to treat each other with consideration and courtesy, and to cheerfully accept each other's faults as well as their good qualities.

2   Healthcare

Exam focus: Completing tables and diagrams
Aims: Working out the meanings of words | Scanning a text for information
Recognising synonyms and antonyms in a text

Part 1:   Vocabulary

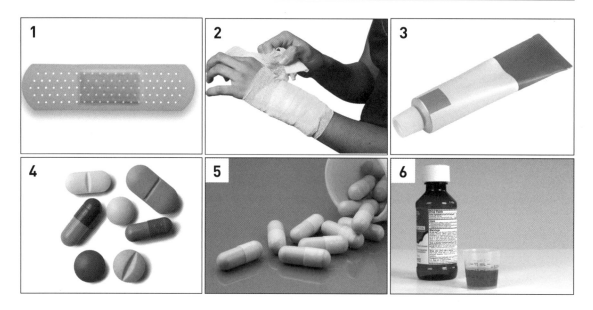

1   Match the pictures 1–6 above with the words a–f.

a   a bandage _____   **c**   cream _____   **e**   syrup _____
b   capsules _____   **d**   a plaster _____   **f**   tablets _____

2   Match the words 1–6 to the definitions a–f.

1 a cuff _____	a an instrument that a doctor uses to listen to your heart and breathing
2 a jab _____	b a small device that helps you to breathe more easily if you have asthma or a bad cold. You put it in your mouth and breathe in deeply, and it sends a small amount of a drug into your lungs.
3 a stethoscope _____	c a small tube with a thin hollow needle at the end, used for injecting drugs or for taking blood from someone's body
4 a syringe _____	d an instrument for measuring temperature
5 a thermometer _____	e an injection of something into your blood to prevent illness
6 an inhaler _____	f a device used for measuring blood pressure

Exam tip: When you come across a word you don't know in a text, look at the context. It will often express the same idea in other words or give clues as to the meaning.

3 Work out the meaning of the words in italics 1–3 by studying their context in the passage below.

Many parents would not know what to do if their child fell and banged their head, (1) *choked* on a small toy or scalded themselves on a hot iron, research shows. The British Red Cross organisation, which (2) *commissioned* the survey, is so alarmed by the findings that it has created a cheap and easy computer-based training programme for parents called 'learn first aid fast'. The charity's first aid specialist said that learning basic rescue and recovery techniques could be the most important thing any parent did. About one million children under fifteen are admitted to accident and emergency (3) *units* every year after accidents in the home.

1 choke

  a to hit with a lot of force
  b to be unable to breathe because something is blocking the air passage to your lungs
  c to have health problems

2 commission

  a to order or authorize the production of something
  b to like something
  c to make a decision based on facts

3 unit

  a a department
  b a large number of something
  c a medical test

4 For each of the words in italics 1–4 in the passage below, find a synonym or antonym in the same sentence.

Accidents are the main reason for deaths in children aged more than twelve months, accounting for nearly 400 (1) *fatalities* a year. Falls are the most common accident, accounting for forty-three per cent of accidental injury to children at home. Burns are common, too, with ten children under five getting burnt or (2) *scalded* every day.

'Some people appear to be reassured by owning a first aid (3) *kit*, but if they are going to help someone then they must have first aid knowledge and skills as well as equipment,' a first aid specialist said. The results of the Red Cross survey revealed alarming levels of (4) *ignorance*, with many parents relying more on stories than on knowledge or common sense when faced with an emergency.

Exam tip: When you learn the meaning of a word which often occurs in academic texts, it is a good idea to look up and learn the different word forms as well.

5 Complete the table.

Verb	Noun
1 _____	a commission
to survey	2 _____
3 _____	a recovery
to injure	4 _____
5 _____	equipment
to aid	6 _____
7 _____	ignorance

Part 2:   Practice exercises

 Exam information: Completion tasks (1)
Completion tasks test your ability to find and understand detailed or specific information in a text.

Completing a table, diagram, or picture: You will have to read a passage and complete a table, diagram, or picture. The information in the passage will not necessarily be in the same order as the questions. The table, diagram, or picture may relate to a section of the passage rather than the whole.

You will be told how many words you should use (e.g. no more than two words, one word only, no more than two words and a number). Numbers can be written in numbers (e.g. *5*) or words (e.g. *five*). Hyphenated words count as one word (e.g. *state-of-the-art* counts as one word).

Exam tip: When you are looking for specific information (e.g. places, names, phrases), move your eyes down the text, looking only for words and phrases related to the information you want. Do not read word for word, do not stop if there are words you do not know, and ignore any information you do not need. This technique is called 'scanning'. You can also use the text style or formatting to help you. Sometimes, numbers, uppercase letters, italics, bold print, quotation marks and other visual information within a text can help you locate the information you want.

1   Scan the passage below to find information about the topics 1–7 in the table. There are clues to help you find the information. The first one has been done for you.

Questions	Clues	Specific information
What is another name for the Beveridge Report?	Look for capital letters; find the words 'Beveridge Report' and scan the text around 'Beveridge Report'.	1 Report on Social Insurance
Date of report:	Scan the text for a four-digit number, which is how years are usually expressed.	2 _____
What was the subject of the report?	Look at the name of the report.	3 _____ _____
How many obstacles to progress did the report mention?	Scan the text for a number expressed in digits or in words.	4 _____ _____
What were the obstacles to progress?	Look for a bulleted list.	5 _____ _____
What is 'Squalor'?	Scan the text for 'Squalor' and read the words in brackets: they explain the meaning.	6 _____ _____
Why was the report commissioned?	Scan the text for forms of the words 'commission', 'reason' or 'why'.	7 _____ _____

The 1940s saw the development of legislation that reflected an agreement across the main political parties that the state should take an increased responsibility for the funding and provision of welfare services. The specific measures taken were based on the proposals of Sir William Beveridge (1879–1963) and published in his *Report on Social Insurance* (1942), more commonly known as the Beveridge Report. Beveridge based his recommendations on his concern to defeat five 'giant evils' that, despite earlier measures, were still hindering social and economic progress in Britain. These were:

- Want (poverty)
- Disease (ill health and high mortality rates)
- Ignorance (inadequate education)
- Squalor (poor housing and homelessness)
- Idleness (unemployment)

The existence of poverty in Britain was the underlying reason for commissioning the report, but legislation was passed and services introduced that addressed each of the 'five giants'.

2 Scan the passage below about vulnerable people in society (i.e. those people who are in more danger of being harmed, physically or emotionally, than others). Then complete the table with notes.

Care for vulnerable people
State responsibility:
Support from the church:

1 In all societies there are groups of people who are potentially vulnerable. These include children, older people, people with disabilities, and the poor, for example. Whether they are supported and how they are supported, however, varies from society to society and at different times in history.

2 In some societies, the care of the vulnerable is seen as the responsibility of the family or the village. In others, it is principally the responsibility of the state, through community provision. In Israeli kibbutzim*, for example, the care of children is seen as the responsibility of the whole community, and not principally the concern of the birth parents. In other societies the care of children is the prime responsibility of their parents, and in some it is the responsibility of the extended family. Attitudes to the vulnerable vary. Those on benefits may be seen as 'lazy scroungers', or their situation may be seen as the result of poor parenting or the inevitable consequence of economic changes. The response to their need will vary according to the dominant attitudes in the society, the views and priorities of government, the wealth of the nation, and how that wealth is distributed and managed.

3 In England, the state has had some involvement in providing for the poor since Elizabethan times. The 1601 Poor Law allowed officials to collect money from each household in their parish and to distribute it to the needy. However, it was thought that the poor only had themselves to blame. The political approach at the time was informed by a view that the government should not interfere in the workings of the economy or in the provision of welfare services. The church and other voluntary groups provided charitable support, but the state 'left well alone'. Not until the opening years of the twentieth century did the state begin to take a proactive role in the care and welfare of its citizens.

Glossary:
kibbutzim: (singular: kibbutz) communal settlements, typically farms in Israel

3   Look at the passage in Exercise 2. Write a sentence for each of the three paragraphs, summarising what its function is. The first one has been done for you.

Paragraph 1: This introduces the topic of vulnerable people (and the support they receive) by giving a definition.

4   Imagine that you need to find information in the passage in Exercise 2 about the topics 1–4 below. Do not read the text again but use the summaries you wrote in Exercise 3 to decide in which paragraph you should look for the answer.

  1 What do people think of 'vulnerable' people? Paragraph _____

  2 What does 'vulnerable' mean? Paragraph _____

  3 What support was provided in the twentieth century in England? Paragraph _____

  4 Who is responsible for the care of vulnerable people? Paragraph _____

> **Exam tips:**
>
> - When you do a completion task, read the instructions carefully and note how many words you are allowed to write. Sometimes you will have to summarise the information in order to keep within the word limit.
> - Charts or diagrams give a summary of the information and show visual links, so think about the relationship between the ideas in a text. The different parts of a chart/diagram may not be in the same order as the information in the text. The chart/diagram may not show all the information included in the text.
> - The answers in a particular section of the chart/diagram must belong to the same grammatical category, e.g. they should all be nouns, or all verbs.
> - The chart/diagram may not use the same words as the text but synonyms or paraphrases.

5   Scan the passage below and complete the diagram with the missing information. Write NO MORE THAN FOUR WORDS in each box.

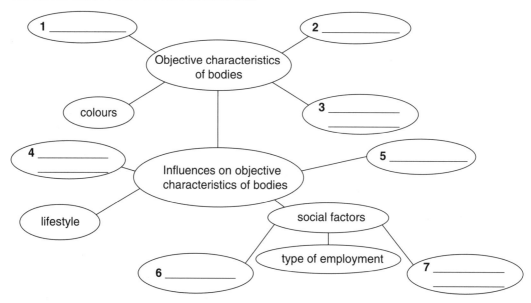

So far in this chapter, we have questioned common-sense ideas held about what is sickness and health and have raised some challenging questions about these ideas. However, we can go further and question a closely related concept upon which notions of illness are ultimately based: the concept of 'the body'.

All of us exist in 'bodies' that are objectively different shapes, heights, colours and physical abilities; they are also subjectively valued as attractive or ugly, young or old, short or tall, weak or strong.

Let us look first at the objective differences. The two most common explanations for objective differences between bodies are, first, that people's bodies vary according to genetic differences (height, weight, etc.) and, second, that bodies change as people age. However, sociologists point out that the shapes of people's bodies are often actually linked to diets, type of employment and general quality of life. A huge range of research indicates that poorer people are more likely to:

- eat 'unhealthy' foods and to smoke cigarettes
- be employed in repetitive, physically demanding work or the other extreme of boring, sedentary employment
- have worse housing conditions
- live in more deprived neighbourhoods

All of these factors impact upon the condition of a person's body and health. We can see then that the physical shapes of bodies are strongly influenced by social factors.

6   Scan the passage below and complete the table with the missing information 1–8. The first one has been done for you.

Legislation (laws)	Type of payment	For whom?
1 The Family Allowance Act 1945	financial payment	2
3	<ul><li>unemployment benefit</li><li>sickness benefit</li><li>retirement pension</li><li>maternity benefit</li><li>widow's pension</li></ul>	4
5	6	people who did not pay into the national insurance scheme and did not receive those benefits
7	free health services at the point of delivery, based on need	8

The Family Allowance Act 1945 introduced a financial payment for children under 15. This did not apply for the first child but applied for all subsequent children.

The National Insurance Act 1946 allowed for the payment of unemployment benefit, sickness benefit and retirement pension, maternity benefit and widow's pension for all who, when in work, paid weekly from their wages into the national insurance scheme.

The National Assistance Act 1948 provided a 'safety net' – a minimum income for people who did not pay into the national insurance scheme and were, therefore, not eligible for those benefits.

The National Health Service Act 1948. Before the introduction of the National Health Service (NHS), if people needed to see a doctor or have hospital treatment they normally had to pay. A national service was central to the post-war welfare reforms and was based on three principles:
1   That health services should be free to all at the point of delivery (when they are actually used).
2   That the service would be truly national, covering the whole population in all parts of the country.
3   That access to services would be based on clinical need (not on the ability to pay).

Part 3: Exam practice

Complete the tables on the next page.

Choose NO MORE THAN THREE WORDS from the passage for each answer.

The rising problem of obesity has helped to make diabetes treatments the biggest drug bill in primary care, with almost £600 million of medicines prescribed by doctors last year, according to the NHS Information Centre.

Analysts said that young people contracting the condition, which is often associated with obesity, were helping to push up costs as doctors tried to improve their long-term control of the disease and prevent complications.

A total of 32.9 million diabetes drugs, costing £599.3 million, were prescribed in the past financial year. In 2004–05 there were 24.8 million, costing £458 million. More than 90 per cent of the 2.4 million diabetics in England have type 2 diabetes, with the remainder suffering from type 1, the insulin-dependent form of the disease. There are thought to be 500,000 undiagnosed cases of diabetes.

While rates of type 1 have shown slight increases in recent years, type 2 has risen far more rapidly — a trend linked to the increasing number of people who are overweight or obese. Almost one in four adults in England is obese, with predictions that nine in ten will be overweight or obese by 2050. Obesity costs the NHS £4.2 billion annually. This year the Government started a £375 million campaign aimed at preventing people from becoming overweight by encouraging them to eat better and exercise more.

An NHS Information Centre spokeswoman who worked on the report, which was published yesterday, said that diabetes was dominating the primary care drug bill as better monitoring identified more sufferers and widely used medications for other conditions such as statins became cheaper. She said that the data suggested a growing use of injectable insulin in type 2 diabetes care, which was helping to push up costs.

Doctors agreed that more expensive long-acting insulin, which can cost about £30 per item, was being used more often, as well as more expensive pills and other agents.

The report, an update of the centre's June publication *Prescribing for Diabetes in England*, shows that the number of insulin items prescribed last year rose by 300,000 to 5.5 million, at a total cost of £288.3 million. It marked an 8 per cent rise on the £267 million spent in the previous year. However, while the number of anti-diabetic drugs, which are mostly in tablet form, also rose, the cost dropped slightly to £168.1 million.

'Type 2 is increasing. We are seeing it in younger people, and because it is a progressive disease, people are needing an increasing number of interventions as time goes by,' the spokeswoman said, adding that long-acting insulins such as Glargine were now common. 'For people who are struggling to control their type 2 diabetes it makes sense, but it is quite a big clinical change from five or ten years ago.'

Other anti-diabetic items, such as use of the subcutaneous injection exenatide, have also increased and cost £14.3 million. Laurence Buckman, chairman of the British Medical Association's general practice committee, said that he had observed a trend with drugs such as exenatide, which costs £80 per item. He said that younger patients could start on cheaper tablets such as metformin, which costs £3.70 per box, but were needing increasingly sophisticated treatments to keep their condition in check.

'You are talking about an ever larger number of people getting a large range of drugs to reduce long-term complications. Type 2 is a common chronic illness that is getting commoner. It's in everyone's interest to treat people early and with the most effective drugs, and these are the more expensive tablets and long-acting insulins,' he said.

Glossary:
primary care: health care provided in the community, e.g. when people make a first appointment with a doctor
insulin: a hormone produced in the pancreas (an organ in the body) which regulates the amount of glucose (a type of sugar) in the blood.
Lack of insulin causes a form of diabetes.
obese: very overweight
subcutaneous: applied under the skin

Exam tip: For some texts there may be a glossary for words that IELTS candidates are not expected to know or have come across before. It is a good idea to check if difficult or technical terms are explained here.

Name of drug	Cost per item
insulin	1
exenatide	2
metformin	3

Total for ...	Cost of medicine in million pounds
diabetes last year	4
diabetes 2004–5	458
insulin last year	5
insulin 2 years ago	6

3 Getting an education

Exam focus: Answering short-answer questions
Aims: Working out meaning from context | Recognising key words in a sentence
Finding and understanding specific information | Keeping to the word limit
Taking notes

Part 1: Vocabulary

1   The pictures above show items of school uniform that parents in Britain may have to buy
for their children. Match the pictures 1–6 with the words a–f.

a	a blazer _____	**c**	a gingham dress _____	**e**	pumps _____
b	a cardigan _____	**d**	a pinafore dress _____	**f**	tracksuit bottoms _____

2   Match the words 1–7 to the definitions a–g.

1	a compass _____	a	a flat, semi-circular piece of plastic or metal which is used for measuring angles
2	a test tube _____	b	an area of land that contains the main buildings of a university or college
3	a protractor _____	c	a building with rooms or flats, usually built by universities or colleges, in which students live during the term
4	a laboratory _____	d	a hinged V-shaped instrument that you use for drawing circles

5 a hall of residence ____	e a small tube-shaped container made from glass, used in laboratories
6 a lectern ____	f a room containing scientific equipment where students are taught science subjects such as chemistry
7 a campus ____	g a high sloping desk on which someone puts their notes when they are standing up and giving a lecture

3   Underline at least five words or phrases related to the topic of education in the following text. Use your dictionary if necessary.

If you send your child to a boarding school you can be looking at fees of almost £8,000 per term. Eton will charge £7,896 a term from September – a rise of 5.8% on last year's fees. Winchester's fees have gone up 5% from £7,457 to £7,833 a term. Day schools are cheaper, but even these are charging an average of £2,796 a term – £8,388 a year.

If you have a baby this year and plan to send him or her to a private day school for secondary education, it will set you back about £150,000, according to an independent adviser.

If your child is starting senior school this September, the school fees between 11 and 18 will total an average of £75,500, assuming the fees rise by 7% a year.

4   Match the words 1–10 with the definitions a–j.

1 a day school ____	a a school for pupils between the ages of 11 or 12 and 17 or 18
2 a special needs school ____	b a school for children between the ages of 5 and 11
3 a boarding school ____	c a school suitable for the majority of children
4 a mainstream school ____	d a school in Britain for children aged between 11 and 18 who have a high academic ability
5 a secondary/senior school ____	e a state school in which children of all abilities are taught together
6 a private school (Britain) ____	f a school for children who need special help or care, for example because they are physically or mentally disabled
7 a college ____	g a school which is not supported financially by the government and which parents have to pay for their children to go to
8 a primary school ____	h a school where the students go home every evening and do not live at the school
9 a grammar school ____	i an institution where students study after they have left school
10 a comprehensive school ____	j a school which some or all of the pupils live in during the school term

5 Answer the questions 1–7. Use your dictionary if necessary.

1 If you cram for an examination, you are learning as much as possible in a short time just before you take the examination. Do you normally cram for an exam, or do you plan your revision carefully?

2 When you graduate from university, you have successfully completed a degree course. Do you know anyone who has recently graduated?

3 When you qualify, you pass the examinations that you need to be able to work in a particular profession. Do you know anyone who has recently qualified as a doctor or a lawyer?

4 In Britain, you can take GCSE exams when you are sixteen. Do you know what GCSE stands for?

5 If a pupil is expelled from school, they are officially told to leave because they have behaved badly. If a pupil is suspended, they are asked to leave for a certain period of time because they have behaved badly, but they can then come back. Can you give examples of bad behaviour in school that may lead to a student being suspended or expelled?

6 In Britain, a reception class is a class that children go into when they first start school at the age of four or five. How old are children when they start school in your country?

7 A truant is a pupil who stays away from school without permission. How were truants punished at your school?

6 Work out the meaning of the words and phrases in italics 1–6 by studying their context in the passage below.

A grandmother has set up her own school to cater for her autistic grandson. Joshua, 7, was unable to cope at the local school and his parents were struggling to get his needs met.

'I used to take Joshua to his mainstream school,' says his mother. 'He would literally (1) *howl* all the way down the very long drive. I used to feel like a monster.'

She took Joshua out of the school on the advice of his teachers, but (2) *hit a brick wall* with the local education authority, who wanted to place him in a school for 90 children with a huge range of learning difficulties — contrary to the modern expertise on (3) *autism*, which recommends specialist care in small units.

Now, Joshua is (4) *flourishing* in a small school for autistic youngsters. 'It is costing us £15,000 a year but it's worth it to see Joshua making progress. He is a different child.'

The special needs school recently passed its first inspection from the Office for Standards in Education with a (5) *glowing* report. Despite this, the education authority has refused to pay for Joshua's education there.

Receiving a diagnosis of a learning disability is a terrible blow to families, and the realisation that you face years of fighting to obtain the education that will help your child is (6) *devastating*. Many parents cannot face the struggle and many children are denied the chance to improve their quality of life.

1 howl
 a cry loudly to express pain or unhappiness
 b sing loudly
 c run quickly

2 hit a brick wall
 a have an accident
 b agree about most things
 c be unable to make progress

3 autism
 a a type of mental condition, present from early childhood
 b a type of cold or flu
 c a mental illness characterised by a refusal to eat

4 flourishing
 a flowering
 b developing rapidly and successfully
 c studying

5 glowing
 a satisfactory
 b expressing approval
 c with an intense colour and shine

6 devastating
 a difficult in the beginning
 b not pleasant
 c causing shock or distress

7 Complete the table with words from the passages in Exercises 3 and 6.

Verb	Noun	Adjective
1 _____	an assumption	—
2 _____	a rise	—
—	3 _____	expert
—	4 _____	young
to progress	5 _____	progressive
to inspect	6 _____	—
to diagnose	7 _____	diagnostic
to realise	8 _____	—

Part 2: Practice exercises

Exam information: Short-answer questions

In this task type, you are asked about factual details. The task tests your ability to find and understand specific information in a text. Your answers will consist of no more than a certain number of words or numbers. Note:

- Numbers can be written as words (e.g. *eight*) or figures (e.g. 8).
- Hyphenated words count as one word (e.g. *merry-go-round*).

The questions are normally in the same order as the information in the text. In other words, the answer to question 1 occurs in the text before the answer to question 2, and so on.

1 How many words are there in the sentences 1–4 below?

1 Describe the habitat of the orang-utan.
2 'The fact that two major designers have included blue-black jeans in their summer range does not make them fashion.' Discuss.
3 Outline the rights of old-age pensioners in society, especially the over-seventies.
4 Evaluate the availability of over-the-counter medicines.

2 Answer the questions 1–8 in no more than three words.

1 How did you use to travel to school?
2 Do you remember the name of your first school teacher?
3 Name your three favourite subjects in secondary school.
4 What is your favourite memory of your time at school?
5 Give an example of a negative experience you had in school.
6 Describe the type of food you used to eat at school.
7 Have you ever failed an exam or test?
8 What would you like to study at college or university?

> **Exam tip:** If you cannot find an answer to a question, go to the next one. If you find the answer to that question, you will know that you need to go back in the text to find the answer to the previous one.

3 The questions 1–4 are about the text below. They should be in the same order as the information in the text but they have been mixed up. Put the questions in the right order. You do not have to answer them.

1 Money is only one consideration for politicians. Give evidence from the text to show this.
2 Illustrate how celebrities can influence politicians.
3 Give examples from the text of different types of policies.
4 Apart from celebrities, which other forces can influence politicians?

Policies can be influenced by many forces. For example, Jamie Oliver's TV programme, *Jamie's School Dinners*, attacking the quality of food in schools, eventually persuaded the Minister for Education to rethink policies about the eating habits of children, as well as budgets. Equally so, very large organisations with a global presence influence policy makers all around the world over concerns such as oil, arms, the environment and human rights.

4 Skim-read the passage and decide what type of information is in each paragraph. Make short notes about this information.

1 Plans to allow universities to charge unlimited tuition fees were today greeted with dismay from students and lecturers but welcomed by vice-chancellors at top-flight institutions. Fees of up to £6,000 a year would go directly to universities, but above that figure they would pay a levy that would increase for each additional £1,000, restricting the extra income, under proposals set out by a review of higher education funding. Graduates would also repay their loans later and over a longer period.

2 Lord Browne of Madingley proposed a new system under which one graduate in five in lower-paid jobs would repay less than today but higher-earning graduates would pay more. His proposals, following a review of higher education finance lasting almost a year, will form the basis of a new system for funding universities from autumn 2012. 'Under these plans universities can start to vary what they charge,' he said, 'but it will be up to students whether they choose the university. The money will follow the student, who will follow the quality. The student is no longer taken for granted, the student is in charge.'

3 Aaron Porter, president of the National Union of Students said: 'If adopted, Lord Browne's review would hand universities a blank cheque and force the next generation to pick up the tab for devastating cuts to higher education. The only thing students and their families would stand to gain from higher fees would be higher debts. A market in course prices between universities would increasingly put pressure on students to make decisions based on cost rather than academic ability or ambition.'

4 The review recommends:

- Graduates would not start to repay student loans until they earn £21,000 a year. This threshold would rise in line with earnings to protect graduates with lower incomes. The current threshold is £15,000.
- Repayments would stay at 9 per cent of income but graduates with higher earnings would pay a higher interest rate of 2.2 per cent above inflation, equal to the Government's cost of borrowing. Lower-paid graduates would continue to pay no real interest rate on loans.
- Student loans would be paid over a maximum of 30 years, after which they would be written off. The current maximum is 25 years.
- Student support should be simplified, with a flat living loan of £3,750 for all undergraduates and maintenance grants of up to £3,250. Full grants would go to students whose family income was £25,000 or less and partial grants to those with household income up to £60,000.

5 Professor Steve Smith, president of Universities UK, which represents vice-chancellors, said: 'We are extremely pleased that Lord Browne's proposals build on the fair and progressive elements of the current system. No parent or student would have to pay tuition fees upfront, only a graduate would pay when they are earning £21,000 per year. This will be crucial in supporting those from disadvantaged backgrounds through university.'

6 But union leaders and representatives of newer universities warned of the 'devastating' impact on families if the recommendations are implemented. Professor Les Ebdon, chair of million+, which represents new universities, said: 'There is a real risk that some students who would have gone to university will decide not to go and that opportunity and social mobility will be fatally undermined.'

7 Lord Browne, the former group chief executive of BP, said that despite higher fees the number of people going to university should expand. His plans allow for a 10 per cent increase in the number of student places over the next four years. Part-time students would also have access to student loans to cover the cost of their tuition fees, giving more people a second chance to study for a degree later in life, he said. His plans would create a market in higher education, with many research universities likely to charge £6,000 or £7,000 a year, a handful of top universities charging higher fees, but many newer universities that focus on teaching charging less.

Paragraph 1: Introduction of the plans

Paragraph 2: _____

Paragraph 3: _____

Paragraph 4: _____

Paragraph 5: _____

Paragraph 6: _____

Paragraph 7: _____

5 **Look at the following question about the passage in Exercise 4 above.**

> From the point of view of students, what would be the negative consequences of higher tuition fees?

Which of the strategies 1–6 do you think would be useful to find the answer?

1 underlining the important information in the text
2 underlining the key words in the questions
3 reading the text before reading the questions
4 reading the questions slowly before reading the text
5 numbering the paragraphs in the text
6 scanning the text (moving your eyes down over the text to find the information you are looking for, without reading the text word for word)

Exam tip: In order to find the correct answer in a text, focus on what you are looking for. One way to do that is to think about the key words in the questions.

Example: What is your favourite memory of your time in school?

The question word ('What') is important. The nouns ('memory' and 'school') also carry a lot of information. Words like 'your' and 'of' are not necessary to understand the question. Note that 'time' is not a key word: the question asks about memories, not time.

6   Underline the key words or phrases in the questions 1–10.

1   Who is against the proposed changes to student tuition fees?
2   How could a future loan repayment schedule be described in comparison to today's?
3   According to the official statement from the National Union of Students, who will suffer financially?
4   From the point of view of students, what would be the negative consequences of higher tuition fees?
5   In the future, what may become the deciding factor for students choosing a university?
6   What will happen to the maximum period of repayment?
7   What will students whose parents earn a total of £55,000 receive?
8   According to Universities UK, who would especially benefit from the new system?
9   According to newer universities, what might happen to the number of people who are able to move up in society?
10 Who may ask for fees of over £7,000?

7   As quickly as you can, find the answers to the questions 1–10 in Exercise 6 by referring to the text on pages 29 and 30. Then answer the questions in no more than three words.

8   Read the questions 1–10 and the answers one student found in a passage. In order for her answers to be valid, the answers must be expressed in no more than three words. Rewrite the answers. The first one has been done for you.

Questions	Student's answers	Short answers
1 How much do they need to pay?	They need to pay £6,000 per year.	£6,000 annually
2 How will students finance their education?	With a combination of loans and salaries from part-time jobs.	
3 How did the university react to the news?	They immediately released a statement to the press.	
4 What are the disadvantages of cramming?	There is a possibility that students will become too tired.	
5 Give one reason why students might want to choose accommodation on campus?	It is closer to their place of study.	
6 What do students need to do before they can qualify as a lawyer?	They need to complete a course that lasts for four years.	
7 What do parents consider when they choose a school?	They look at a number of different factors: location, cost and school results.	

8 What are the advantages of home schooling?	The lessons are planned with individual students in mind and the teachers know the students very well.	
9 Why is it a good idea to send children to nursery school?	The children develop their ability to be social.	
10 Give a reason why some students have been punished.	They had a mobile phone on them.	

Exam tip: It can be difficult to limit your answers to three words. Sometimes it can help to change a verb to a noun, or to use nouns as adjectives.

9 Rewrite the answers 1–9 in no more than three words. Do not use any verbs in your answers.

Example: *Question: What sort of technical difficulties has the school been having?*
Answer: There have been problems with the systems that are currently used by the computers.
<u>*computer system problems*</u>

1 Q: What idea has the Head Teacher come up with?
A: Her idea is to adapt the way the college communicates.

_____

2 Q: What action do they need to take first?
A: They need to correct the information in the timetables.

_____

3 Q: What is even more urgent than improving communications?
A: They need to find methods to help them save time.

_____

4 Q: Name one of the aims that are mentioned on the final list.
A: The school library wants to increase the number of books it lends out.

_____

5 Q: What is the main priority in terms of after-school activities?
A: They would like to put on plays during term time only.

_____

6 Q: What else would they like to increase?
A: They also aim to do more sports activities after school.

_____

7 Q: What is the school satisfied with?
A: They are happy with the way they keep control of their resources.

_____

8 Q: What aspect of the school's performance still needs to be determined?
A: They need to assess how satisfied the students are.

_____

Part 3:   Exam practice

Using NO MORE THAN THREE WORDS for each, answer the following questions.

1   Why do private providers feel they need to pay as much as children's centres?

_____

2   What is the most a senior nursery nurse could earn?

_____

3   Out of all children, how many take up places in private nurseries?

_____

4   What types of nurseries do fathers and mothers prefer?

_____

Parents face a sharp increase in nursery fees from January as new government-subsidised children's centres drive up staff costs for private daycare.

Children's centres are offering up to £7,000 a year more for managers and nursery nurses to staff their premises, forcing private providers to match the pay offer or risk losing their best employees. Fees are private nurseries' only source of income so they have no option but to pass on the 12–15 per cent salary increases to parents. Salaries account for 80 per cent of running costs and fees are an average of £140 a week.

The annual pay survey for *Nursery World* magazine found that the salary of a nursery manager in the private sector had risen by an average of 12.3 per cent this year, to £21,547, as owners attempted to hang on to their staff. Despite the increase, children's centres are offering about £27,000 for a manager. Senior nursery nurses have had an average 17 per cent increase this year, with salaries of about £14,000, but could still earn up to £17,000 if they switched to a children's centre.

'Children's centres are heavily subsidised and are offering much bigger salaries than anywhere else in the sector,' said Claire Schofield, head of membership at the National Day Nurseries Association. 'Shouldn't the subsidy be available across the board?' Private providers currently account for 78 per cent of all nursery places. The Government plans to open 3,500 children's centres by 2010 — five in each parliamentary constituency. Each centre will offer daycare and other services for children and parents. The Department for Education and Skills estimates that the cost of each place will be about £250 a week, well above private sector fees. But a generous subsidy administered by local authorities brings the fees down to about £137 a week.

Liz Roberts, editor of *Nursery World*, predicted that many nurseries would face financial difficulties as a result. 'Nurseries will put up their fees a bit, but there is a limit to what parents can afford so it is becoming terribly difficult. Some nursery owners barely pay themselves as it is, so may just decide to close,' she said.

A Department for Education and Skills study found that only 25 per cent of private nurseries made a profit, with 31 per cent breaking even. While children's centres will offer parents value for money at first, there is no guarantee that the Government will continue to pay the subsidy. If the funding is reduced, parents will have no choice but to pay more for their nursery places, especially if local private nurseries have been driven out of business.

Parents have also made clear during public consultations that they like private and voluntary sector nurseries, which are often smaller and more intimate than local authority providers, and the Government has said that it is committed to diversity of supply.

4 Water

Exam focus: Matching sentence endings
Aims: Developing awareness of sentence structure | Predicting answers
Understanding the main ideas in a text | Reading efficiently
Working with key words and paraphrases

Part 1: Vocabulary

1 Match the pictures 1–6 above with the words a–f.

  a a canal _____   **c** a pond _____   **e** a stream _____
  b a lake _____   **d** a puddle _____   **f** a well _____

2 Match the words 1–10 with the definitions a–j.

1 a dam _____	a an area of calm sea water that is separated from the ocean by a line of rock or sand
2 a drought _____	b a lake that is used for storing water before it is supplied to people
3 a flood _____	c a long line of rocks or sand, the top of which is just above or just below the surface of the sea
4 a lagoon _____	d the ground under the sea
5 a liquid _____	e a bank of sand below the surface of the sea or a river
6 a reef _____	f a substance which is not solid but which flows and can be poured, for example water
7 a reservoir _____	g fine sand, soil, or mud which is carried along by a river
8 a sandbank _____	h a wall that is built across a river in order to stop the water flowing and to make a lake
9 the seabed _____	i a large amount of water that covers an area which is usually dry, for example when a river flows over its banks
10 silt _____	j a long period of time during which no rain falls

3 Match the nouns 1–7 to the words a–g with a similar meaning.

1	sweat ____	a	vapour
2	rain ____	b	purification
3	steam ____	c	perspiration
4	watering ____	d	irrigation
5	cleaning ____ .	e	beverage
6	drink ____	f	immersion
7	dunking ____	g	precipitation

4 Underline at least ten words or phrases related to the topic of liquids in the text below. Use your dictionary if necessary.

> Make a couple of litres of stock from the vegetables. Meanwhile, boil the kettle again and pour the boiling water on the spinach. Then turn up the heat in the pan with the onions, add the rice and toast lightly. Add boiling stock spoon by spoon to the rice. After 15 minutes of gentle simmering, spoon the risotto onto the plates and put a runny fried egg and the spinach on top.
>
> With dessert, pour each person a glass of sweet white wine. Cut a slice of peach into each glass so that you roll fruit and wine together into your mouth – a simple but delicious way to end this meal.

5 Complete the text with the words a–g.

a	beverage	**c**	dunk	**e**	sip	**g**	stir
b	blow	**d**	saucer	**f**	spoon		

> There is an art to having a (1) _____ in one traditional English tearoom in Brighton. You don't put your elbows on the table. You don't make a noise with your (2) _____ on the inside of your cup as you (3) _____ your tea. You don't insult the Queen, (4) _____ from your teaspoon or handle the sugar cubes. And if you use a mobile phone or (5) _____ your biscuit in your tea, you will be invited to leave. There are other rules, too: the cup should be placed back on the (6) _____ between sips and not waved in the air, and you should not (7) _____ on your tea to cool it.

6 Can you list ten sports which can be done on or in water, on ice, or on snow?

7 Underline the correct word in the sentences 1–6.

1 The river *meanders / pours* in great loops along the plain before it reaches the sea.

2 The water *seeped / gushed* out of the burst pipe and soaked the passers-by.

3 I *poured / flowed* him a fresh cup of coffee.

4 It was a very hot day and sweat was *seeping / trickling* slowly down my face.

5 The milk was *seeping / pouring* slowly through the paper carton.

6 The river *flowed / poured* through the valley.

Part 2: Practice exercises

ⓘ **Exam information: Matching sentence endings**

This task tests your ability to understand the main ideas in a text.

You are given a number of incomplete sentences and you need to complete them by choosing from a list of options. There may be more options than you need.

The sentences are based on a text and will be in the same order as the information in the text.

Exam tip: Try to predict how each sentence will end before looking at the list of endings.

1   Look at the sentence beginnings 1–5 below. What kind of word could come next: a noun (or pronoun), a noun phrase (e.g. article + adjective + noun), a gerund, a verb, an adverb, a preposition, a linking word + noun, a linking word + clause? The first one has been done for you.

   1   Small and medium-sized enterprises (SMEs) are responsible for → *noun / noun phrase / gerund* (e.g. *the environment, paying taxes*)

   2   Between 70 and 75 per cent of SMEs are unaware of → ____ / ____ / ____

   3   Unfortunately a lot of small companies don't think about the environment → ____ / ____

   4   In 1994 just 20 per cent of businesses in the UK accepted the link → ____

   5   It is estimated that UK businesses could save a further £3 billion → ____ / ____

2   Match the sentence beginnings 1–8 below with the endings a–h. The predictions you made for some of these in Exercise 1 should help you do this exercise quickly, possibly without reading all of the endings in detail.

1 Small and medium-sized enterprises (SMEs) are responsible for _____	a	and the benefits limited.
2 Between 70 and 75 per cent of SMEs are unaware of _____	b	until something goes wrong and they are in breach of legislation.
3 Small enterprises often complain that they have _____	c	their environmental obligations.
4 Unfortunately, a lot of small companies don't think about the environment _____	d	up to 80 per cent of environmental crimes.
5 Many SMEs also believe that environmental compliance would be too costly _____	e	between environmental performance and profitability.
6 Only few businesses realise how much energy spending could be reduced by doing something simple _____	f	neither the time nor the infrastructure to manage their environmental responsibilities.
7 In 1994 just 20 per cent of businesses in the UK accepted the link _____	g	such as switching off machines that are not in use.
8 It is estimated that UK businesses could save a further £3 billion _____	h	through improved environmental performance.

3 The questions 1–4 are about the text below. They should be in the same order as the information in the text but they have been mixed up. Put the questions in the right order. You do not have to answer them.

1 What would happen in financial terms if more businesses took their environmental obligations seriously?

2 Give an example of a small action that can have big consequences.

3 Give two reasons why small and medium enterprises do not always comply with environmental guidance.

4 What language in the text suggests that it will take a long time before businesses understand the benefits of following environmental guidelines?

Small and medium-sized enterprises (SMEs) are responsible for up to 80 per cent of environmental crimes and more than 60 per cent of the commercial and industrial waste produced in England and Wales, according to research by the Environment Agency. The body says, however, that between 70 and 75 per cent of SMEs are unaware of their environmental obligations. Many SMEs also believe that environmental compliance would be too costly and the benefits limited. Only few businesses realise how much energy spending could be reduced by doing something simple such as switching off machines that are not in use.

While a fundamental shift in business attitudes is desired, agencies like Envirowise are aware that profit incentives may instead be the answer. For instance, Westbury Dairies, in Wiltshire, has introduced a system to collect and reuse condensation formed during the milk evaporation process. This has reduced the demand for mains water by about 90 per cent. Cost savings from purchasing water alone exceed £340,000 per year. But businesses like Westbury Dairies are still in the minority. It is estimated that UK businesses could save a further £3 billion through improved environmental performance.

4 Underline the key words or phrases in the sentence beginnings 1–8.

1 Searching for artefacts under the sea ...

2 The sea, like space, is ...

3 Complex survival equipment must ...

4 The alternative to diving suits and air tanks is ...

5 The expedition was a cover story ...

6 One of the most important things that an archaeologist will need in searching the seabed is ...

7 Sonar is a tried and tested technology ...

8 Even more problematic than recovering artefacts is ...

> **Exam tip:** In the Reading for IELTS exam, you need to read as efficiently as possible. If you are given more sentence endings than sentence beginnings, read the beginnings because you will need to complete all of them. You will not need all the endings, so only read them when you have to.
>
> Do not be misled by options that are linked to ideas in the passage but are not actually the right answer.

5 Read the sentence beginnings 1–2. Underline the key words and use them to scan the text below each question. Then choose the correct ending a–d.

1 Looking for items under the sea requires

    a hard work on some occasions.
    b an alien environment.
    c a great deal of groundwork.
    d good diving skills.

Searching for artefacts under the sea is some of the most difficult work that archaeologists encounter. The sea, like space, is an alien environment to the human frame. Complex survival equipment must often be donned before archaeologists can make even the first scrape in the seabed.

The alternative to diving suits and air tanks is the submersible, but their use is expensive. Bob Ballard used one to find the *Titanic* in 1985, although he admitted last month that the expedition was a cover story for a mission to find and inspect two sunken nuclear submarines.

One of the most important things that an archaeologist will need in searching the seabed is solid research. Academics and treasure hunters can spend years studying old documents for clues of where best to begin.

2 Finding artefacts

    a has been made easier recently with new sonar technology.
    b was very successful in the sixties.
    c is not as difficult as keeping them in a good condition.
    d was one of William Kidd's activities.

Once the most likely locations have been identified, the business of peering beneath the waves can start. Sonar is a tried and tested technology and among its biggest successes was the discovery of the wreck of the *Mary Rose* in the late sixties. The ship was part of Henry VIII's fleet and sank in the Solent during an engagement with the French in 1545. Archaeologists devoted years to inspecting the wreck, raising a host of artefacts and eventually lifting part of the timber hull to the surface.

Even more problematic than recovering artefacts is preserving them, and archaeologists often need to keep their finds in controlled conditions to prevent disintegration.

In clearer waters divers can search for wrecks just by scouring the seabed. Among such discoveries was that of the *Quedagh Merchant*, Captain William Kidd's ship, in waters only 10ft (3m) deep off Catalina Island in the Dominican Republic.

Exam tip: Do not expect the sentence endings to use the same words as the text. They will probably paraphrase the information in the text.

6 Read the sentence below and note how it can be paraphrased without using the same words.

Example:

> *As cruising becomes ever more international, and as the cultures and holiday traditions of Brits are increasingly confronted with those of Australians, Japanese and Americans, the issue of tipping has become an increasingly controversial minefield.*

Paraphrase: Different cultures have different habits, so now that people from diverse nationalities meet on cruise ships more and more, it is difficult to agree on what to do about tipping.

Now read the sentences 1–3 and choose the better paraphrase, a or b.

> **1** A recent newspaper story reported that Britain's cruise ship travellers are becoming increasingly hostile to the practice of tipping.

    a According to an article, tipping is getting less popular with cruise passengers.
    b The newspapers have suggested that a large number of passengers hate tipping.

> **2** The rise of more dining venues and styles has represented a major change in the cruise tradition of tipping.

    a The practice of tipping on cruises is changing because of the larger variety of eating arrangements.
    b The increase of larger dining venues and methods has meant a big adaptation of cruise tipping traditions.

> **3** Cruise passengers also resent the implication that they should, beyond paying for a cruise to begin with, further be required to supplement crew salaries.

    a Cruise passengers don't like being accused of not paying enough to the cruise personnel in the first place.
    b Cruise ship travellers do not like the idea that on an already expensive holiday they are also expected to contribute to the staff's wages.

7 Look at the topics in the sentence beginnings a–d. In which paragraphs of the passage below can you find information about them?

    a Rising sea levels ...   Paragraphs: _____, _____,
    b Tsunamis ...   Paragraphs: _____, _____, _____, _____
    c Giant waves ...   Paragraphs: _____, _____, _____, _____, _____, _____
    d Water sports ...   Paragraphs: _____, _____

Giant Waves: Exhilaration and Devastation

1 Laird Hamilton, Brett Lickle and a small group of their surfer friends are among the first people ever to ride waves higher than 40 feet. They created the sport of tow surfing – dragging people onto big waves with jet skis or even helicopters – in the early 1990s. 'No one had ridden waves this size,' Hamilton says. 'It was the unknown, like outer space. We didn't know if we were going to come back.'

2 Of the two men, the better known is Hamilton, 46, who has worked as a model, actor, stunt double (for Pierce Brosnan in *Die Another Day*, and Kevin Costner in *Waterworld*) and television presenter. Hamilton and his friends have inspired many others – enthusiasts who tune into weather reports, and catch the first plane to wherever the big waves are expected to hit land. Some of the younger surfers know what they're doing; others – perhaps tempted by a $500,000 prize for anybody who rides a 100-foot wave – are not ready. The fact that ocean waves are getting bigger must be exhilarating for all of them.

3 For the rest of us, however, big waves are very bad news indeed. History is full of examples of devastation being wreaked by waves like these. The biggest wave ever recorded was the one that hit Alaska in 1958, after a huge landslide created a tsunami that peaked at 500 metres above sea level. That's not a misprint: it was more than twice as high as the tallest building in Britain today – Canary Wharf Tower. Scientists know how high it was because the towering wave scraped trees and soil off nearby mountains up to that height.

4 The Alaskan wave is believed to have been a tsunami, caused by a landslide. Italy has been hit by as many as 67 tsunamis in the past 2,000 years, though none with the devastating force of that which killed 230,000 people around the Indian Ocean on Boxing Day 2004.

5 It's useful to distinguish between tsunamis, which are caused by geological events (such as landslides or earthquakes), and giant waves generated by weather, such as those Hamilton and Lickle ride, or the water deposited on New Orleans by Hurricane Katrina. But it is anticipated that both types will become a lot more common as a result of worldwide global warming.

6 According to the Intergovernmental Panel on Climate Change, the oceans now absorb more than 80 per cent of the heat added to the climate system. As the waters heat up, wind velocity increases, storm tracks become more volatile, polar ice and glaciers melt, and sea levels rise.

7 Everything in the oceans seems to be rising: wave heights, sea levels, surface temperatures, wind speeds, storm intensities, coastal surges, tsunami risks. 'Now is the time to prepare for great floods,' a July 2009 editorial in *New Scientist* advised. 'The future of the UK's coastal cities is in jeopardy due to rising sea levels,' reported Lloyd's. Similarly, nine out of the world's ten largest cities are located on low-lying coastal land.

8 And it's not only on land that higher seas and bigger waves pose a threat. Merchant shipping carries around 90 per cent of international trade, on approximately 50,000 boats worldwide, with crew numbers of around a million. Over the past decade, around 100 ships with a cargo capacity of 500 gross tons have been lost each year, or damaged beyond repair – the equivalent of two large ships every week.

9 But this is not new. For centuries, sailors told of the existence of monstrous waves up to 100 feet high that could appear without warning in mid-ocean, against the prevailing current and wave direction, and often in perfectly clear and calm weather. Such waves were said to consist of an almost vertical wall of water preceded by a trough so deep that it was referred to as a 'hole in the sea'. Scientists were sceptical, until the existence of freak waves was confirmed in 1995 in Norway, where an 84-foot wave occurred amid seas where the average of the tallest 33 per cent of waves was 39 feet. This wave changed everything: the emphasis shifted from explaining why freak waves were impossible, to figuring out why they occurred in the first place.

8 Match the four topics a–d in Exercise 7 above with the sentence endings 1–12. Find evidence in the passage for your answers. Be careful: there is one sentence ending that does not relate to any of the topics.

Example: ... *are still being invented. d:* 'They created the sport of tow surfing'

1 ... threaten many cities. ____
2 ... can involve helicopters. ____
3 ... have occurred in Norway. ____
4 ... can be caused by earthquakes. ____
5 ... are popular with TV presenters. ____
6 ... are caused by increasing temperatures. ____

7 ... can be caused by a hurricane. ____
8 ... can appear suddenly. ____
9 ... are both dangerous and fun. ____
10 ... are caused by weather. ____
11 ... can be caused by landslides. ____
12 ... can be predicted. ____

Part 3: Exam practice

*Complete each sentence with the correct endings **A–F** from the box below. Note that there may be more than one correct ending for each beginning, but that you cannot use all of the endings.*

1 Geothermal Engineering ...

2 The geothermal industry ...

> **A** is focussing on Cornwall because of its tin and copper resources.
> **B** builds power stations underground.
> **C** plans to drill a number of wells.
> **D** can rely on previous research.
> **E** has always been a global business.
> **F** has not proven what it can do yet.

In the coming months, a 170-foot-high drilling rig will transform wasteground near Redruth into a new landmark. The drill belongs to a group that is planning to develop Britain's first commercial-scale geothermal plant on the site. Geothermal Engineering has chosen this part of Cornwall – once renowned for its tin and copper – because of its geology. It sits on a bed of granite whose temperature can reach 200°C. Water will be pumped deep underground and will return to the surface as steam, which will power turbines to generate electricity.

'Cornwall is a real hotspot. It is like someone has put a power station below ground and you are simply tapping into it,' said Ryan Law, founder and managing director of Geothermal Engineering.

Law, a former consultant to the geothermal industry, plans to have three wells at the plant, which together he estimates will produce 10MW of electricity, enough to power 20,000 homes, and 55MW of thermal energy, capable of heating ten hospitals 24 hours a day. The challenge is that the rock is 4.5 kilometres below the earth's surface, meaning that months of precise drilling will be required before any energy is produced. The company has a head start. In 1976, the government-funded Hot Dry Rock Research Project began deep drilling to study the area's geology. Law plans to use the detailed maps the team produced over fifteen years to direct his efforts.

Geothermal energy is not new. The world's first conventional geothermal power station, in southern Tuscany, has been producing electricity for almost 100 years. In Iceland, a quarter of the country's electricity comes from geothermal power. Investment in geothermal projects in Australia is expected to reach $2 billion (£1.3 billion) by 2014. The industry is also well established in America and Germany. In Britain, schemes are under way in Southampton and Newcastle.

Conventional geothermal power relies on naturally occurring steam pockets near the earth's surface so it tends to be confined to volcanically active regions or areas close to fault lines. Law claims the process his company uses removes this limitation, making the industry viable almost anywhere in the world.

However, despite billions of pounds in public and private investment and a raft of big projects, the industry has so far failed to demonstrate it can fulfil its promise. Critics argue it is costly, reliant on high-risk, time-consuming drilling and struggles to produce large amounts of energy capable of making a real contribution to the world's needs. Law refuses to let such doubts dampen his ambitions. 'What other renewable energy gives you 24-hour supply? The potential is enormous and we are planning another 25 plants.'

Glossary
geothermal: relating to the internal heat of the earth

5 Non-verbal clues

Exam focus: Answering multiple-choice questions
Aims: Locating information in a text | Summarising ideas | Using paraphrases
Identifying incorrect distractors | Using key words and scanning

Part 1: Vocabulary

1   The pictures above are all non-verbal means of communication. Match the pictures 1–6
with their meanings a–f.

a danger of electrocution ＿＿		**d** poisonous substance ＿＿
b level crossing ＿＿		**e** radioactive substance ＿＿
c parking reserved for the disabled ＿＿		**f** pedestrian crossing ＿＿

2   Underline at least ten words or phrases related to the topic of communication in the text
below. Use your dictionary if necessary.

Poor communication between NHS hospitals and care homes may be putting elderly
people at risk of contracting MRSA and other infections, the health and social care
regulator has warned. The Care Quality Commission (CQC) found nearly one in five
homes in England were not being told if patients discharged from hospitals were or had
been infected.

Hospitals are meant to include a written infection history on discharge summaries.
But the survey revealed 17 per cent of care homes said they did not receive information
from hospitals, while another 28 per cent complained of incomplete and illegible data.

Ambulance crews were also often left uninformed. Where there was communication
about patients, it was verbal and not written down. A spokesperson said: 'If we are to tackle
infections effectively we need to check that all providers of care are talking to each other.'

3 Complete the sentences 1–10 with the correct form of the verbs. The verbs all relate to body language.

clap	nod	point	shrug	wave
frown	nudge	shake	smile	wink

1 I could tell she was happy because she was _____.

2 He didn't need to tell me that I didn't get the job. I had already seen him _____ his head.

3 I hate saying goodbye, so I'll just _____ goodbye from the train.

4 Every time she wants to draw my attention to something, she _____ me with her elbow, which I find annoying, and painful, too sometimes.

5 Don't say anything; just _____ if you agree.

6 The audience were delighted with the performance and they wouldn't stop _____ and cheering.

7 I asked them if they knew where my keys were, but they just _____ their shoulders.

8 I knew he was joking: he _____ at me before he told us the news.

9 _____ at people with your finger is impolite.

10 I wasn't expecting a good mark; the teacher was _____ while she was reading my essay.

4 Look at the phrases 1–8. Write P if the phrase has a positive connotation and N if it has a negative one.

1 to hug someone _____ 5 to stroke someone _____

2 to glare at someone _____ 6 to tickle someone _____

3 to kick someone _____ 7 to slap someone _____

4 to kiss someone _____ 8 to stare at someone _____

5 Match the sentence fragments 1–7 with the sentence fragments a–g.

1 When the company asked me to sign the form, I didn't realise I was signing _____	a up for the army.
2 I have to stay home because I need to sign _____	b in before they can go upstairs.
3 I've decided what I want to do in the future: I'm going to sign _____	c on the dole.
4 My dinner is ready so I need to sign _____	d for a parcel I'm expecting.
5 She lost her job so she's signing _____	e away my rights to compensation.
6 I really need faster internet, so I'm going to sign _____	f off now.
7 All visitors must sign _____	g up for the broadband offer.

Part 2: Practice exercises

 Exam information: Multiple-choice questions

This task tests your ability to understand the main ideas in a text or your understanding of specific points or details.

You will have to choose one answer out of four options, two answers out of five options, or three out of six options. These options may be sentence endings or answers to questions.

The questions will be in the same order as the information in the text.

1 **Answer the questions 1–3 about yourself. You do not have to answer truthfully.**

   1 Have you ever used a social messaging site? Choose one of the four options.

     a never   **c** sometimes
     b once or twice   **d** regularly

   2 Which of the following languages would you like to learn/learn better? Choose two of the five options.

     a Chinese   **c** Spanish   **e** Arabic
     b Japanese   **d** French

   3 Which of the following would you consider signing up for? Choose three of the six options.

     a a social networking site   **c** twitter   **e** a language course at an
     b a free online newspaper   **d** online banking   adult education college
                                                  f an online language course

2 **The questions 1–4 are about the text below. They should be in the same order as the information in the text but they have been mixed up. Put the questions in the right order. You do not have to answer them.**

   1 How important are communication skills in sales?   **3** What is good communication?
   2 What is active listening?   **4** What is good management?

The key to good communication is to pay attention to what other people have to say. Good communicators are definitely not those who like the sound of their own voice. Forget the gift of the gab; communication is all about establishing a rapport with your customers, work colleagues or boss.

The ability to sell is the ultimate test of communication skills. But in the modern world salesmen do not sell, customers choose to buy, says Jon Naylor, the customer service director of PC World. 'You have to empathise with the customer and build a relationship. Listening to the information given and asking the right questions is very important.'

Not listening costs money in the hard world of sales – returned goods, refunds and the loss of repeat custom. But the ability to listen is as important on the top floor as it is on the shop floor and can have just as profound an effect on the bottom line. 'If you ask what makes a good manager, people almost always say "they listen to what we have to say and consider our needs",' says Dr Paul Dobson, a senior lecturer at Cass Business School.

Dr Dobson gives MBA students lessons in 'active listening', which is listening and asking appropriate questions, then clarifying and responding to the answers. 'The fundamental thing is to listen to what people say, which means that you have to be motivated to want to know the answers,' Dr Dobson says.

3 Underline the key words or phrases in the questions 1–4.

   1 Why has it always been difficult to test the idea of a connection between our taste for music and the calls of monkeys?

   2 What do monkeys prefer: music or silence?

   3 Is it true that monkeys appeared to be calmed down by listening to the heavy metal band Metallica?

   4 Who suggested this new kind of experiment to Professor Snowdon?

> **Exam tip:** Once you have identified which section of the text will give you the answer to a multiple choice question, it can be useful to rephrase what it says in that section in your own words: it may help you identify the correct answer more quickly.

4 Summarise the ideas in the short extracts 1–4 in your own words. Try not to use phrases from the text unless absolutely necessary.

Example:

> *The idea that human musical appreciation stems from the same evolutionary root as the vocalisations that primates use to bond and alert others to danger is not new but it has always been hard to test because monkeys do not generally respond to music.*

Summary: Monkeys tend not to react to music, so it is difficult to prove the old belief that our appreciation of music and the calls that monkeys use to communicate have the same evolutionary origin.

   1 When monkeys have been played music, from classical to hard rock, they generally prefer silence. The sole exception has come from one experiment in which monkeys appeared to be calmed down by listening to the heavy metal band Metallica.

   2 However, research carried out by Professor Charles Snowdon of the University of Wisconsin-Madison has shown that cotton-top tamarin monkeys, who normally turn a deaf ear to music, show marked changes in mood when they are played tunes composed with their voices and hearing in mind.

   3 The findings suggest that the historical roots of human appreciation of music may stretch deep into our evolutionary past, to the common ancestors we share with monkeys.

   4 Professor Snowdon took his new experimental approach to the subject at the suggestion of David Teie, who also works at the University of Maryland.

5 Underline the key words in the questions 1–3 and use them to scan the text below. Then answer the questions using bullet points.

   1 What made the sounds on the recorded song for the monkeys in the experiment?

   2 What behaviour did the monkeys display when they were played the 'threat' song?

   3 What happened when the monkeys were played a calming song?

When Mr Teie listened to the calls made by the cotton-top tamarin colony kept at the Wisconsin-Madison psychology department, he immediately recognised emotional states. 'He said, "This is a call from an animal that is upset; this is from an animal that is more relaxed",' Professor Snowdon said.

Mr Teie then used these insights to compose music using features he had noticed in the monkeys' calls, such as rising and falling pitch and the typical length of particular sounds. His aim was to produce 30-second 'songs' that were tuned to the tamarins' musical sense, rather than to the human ear.

The first piece Mr Teie wrote contained rhythmic, staccato beats, based on the type of calls tamarins use to indicate a threat or stress. The second piece featured long, melodic tones, with a descending pitch, that was more like the calming, 'affective' calls the monkeys use during bonding behaviour. All were recorded using the cello and the human voice.

When the monkeys were played the 'threat' song, they moved around more and showed more anxious and social behaviour, all of which are signs of heightened alertness. The monkeys were also more likely to face towards the hidden speaker from which the music was played.

The 'affective' song, by contrast, led to less movement and social behaviour, calmer reactions, and increased feeding – all of which suggest the animals were less stressed and on their guard. Human music that was designed to be calming or threatening produced few reactions among the monkeys.

Monkeys interpret changes in pitch and tone in different ways to humans, but the new research suggests they also use musicality to communicate. Professor Snowdon said: 'People have looked at animal communication in terms of conveying information – "I am hungry" or "I am afraid". But it's much more than that.' He said that monkeys did more than simply convey information. 'I am not calling just to let you know how I am feeling, but my call can also stimulate a similar state in you,' he said. 'That would be valuable if a group was threatened. In that situation, you don't want everybody being calm, you want them alert.'

6   Underline the key words in the questions 1–4 and use them to scan the text below. Then answer the questions using your own words, not words from the text.

1   What is innovative about the predictive texting system that has been developed by Sanjay Patel?

2   What types of hardware and software could work differently in the future because of this invention?

3   What characteristics of the new systems make them so fascinating for the general public?

4   Why is this invention important for Scotland?

'It was so good that my brother, Hash, can type faster than most people using both hands,' said the managing director and founder of KeyPoint Technologies, based in the Innovation Centre, Hillington, Glasgow. 'It helped him use his left hand effectively – and it gave him the confidence to paint again with that hand.'

Hash's accident, which left him disabled, was also the genesis of the software application, written and devised by Sanjay Patel, now 38, that is set to change the way we punch information into our mobile phones and computer keyboards.

Patel and his associates, John Locker, a former games developer, and Dr Mark Dunlop of Strathclyde University and a leading authority on user interface systems, have created AdapTex, a language processing system that cuts down keystroking by around 80%. The software analyses the user's writing patterns and predicts words, cutting down on the number of keystrokes required. It has seen some of the technology industry's biggest players knocking at Patel's door.

'Originally it was an ergonomic idea targeting people with disabilities, but the more research I did, I thought this applies to more than disabled people. The driving force was to reduce the actual physical activity. So in 1997 I started working on creating a piece of software for the mass market that would learn your language traits. It made me realise how inefficient we were when it comes to writing information with e-mail, text messaging, and word-processing on a keyboard. Everybody wants to go faster, so they build the technologies to move faster; what hasn't changed is the human ability to use that technology more effectively,' he said.

'We don't want to change people's practices, we have to complement or improve them. But you can't expect people to change unless you make things better, simpler to use and non-intrusive. I think that's why AdapTex intelligence systems are creating such interest.'

Over the past 15 years, Patel has worked within systems architecture in telecoms and finance. He worked for Nucleus Consulting and project-managed the setting-up of a system for the Merchants' Exchange of St Louis, under the guidance of the Chicago Board of Trade. He completed the two-year contract in a little over a year.

Today Sanjay Patel lives in Partick in Glasgow. Previously from Croydon, he was encouraged to move to Scotland by the prospect of support from Scottish Enterprise, Scottish Development International and by the availability of specialist facilities at the Innovation Centre.

Patel's software takes the predictive text used on mobile phones to the next level: 'A mobile phone is predictive, which uses guesswork, it isn't natural. What we have created is pre-emptive because it is relevant and uses the context. It learns and reshapes itself dynamically. It is about recognition of the patterns you use and is therefore unique to the user. It remodels itself from any document to reflect the author's natural vocabulary, language traits and topics,' he said.

Patel's family arrived in the UK in the 1970s after fleeing from Idi Amin's regime in Uganda. He was brought up in London and, even before his brother's accident, he was fascinated with the science of language patterns. The great selling point is that this pre-empts text in any language because it recognises the patterns,' he said.

Patel is now in discussions with several large international companies interested in incorporating AdapTex into their next-generation computers. 'Some are more cautious than others, but we are on the verge of signing with one of the big PC makers, and hopefully this will mean that they all follow suit,' said Patel.

He is delighted with the support he has been given in Scotland. 'I came because people understood what I was talking about. The business network here, through Global Scot, has given me introductions to the highest levels in the USA. This has been imperative.'

Patel's advisers include John Falconer, a former director of Xerox, who said: 'The market is worth millions and Sanjay could become a very rich man. It could become a significant success story for Scotland.'

7 Using your answers to the questions in Exercise 6 above, choose one correct answer for each question 1–4.

1 What is innovative about the predictive texting system that has been developed by Sanjay Patel?
  a It can help his disabled brother.
  b It uses guesswork.
  c It processes language very fast.
  d It works in a way that is unique to each writer.

2 What types of hardware and software could work differently in the future because of this invention?
  a mobile phones, PCs, e-mail, text messaging, word-processing
  b Adaptex intelligence systems
  c mobile phones and computers
  d telecoms and finance

3 What characteristics of the new systems make them so fascinating for the general public?
  a It completely changes the way people do things.
  b It works with what people already do and makes it better.
  c It can help disabled people.
  d It reduces physical activity.

4 This invention is not just important for Sanjay, his family and the computer business but also for Scotland because
  a the country has made him feel welcome.
  b it has given him financial support.
  c of the business network links with the USA.
  d the country has helped him become successful.

8 Questions 1 and 2 refer to the text in Exercise 6. Choose two correct answers for question 1 and three correct answers for question 2.

1 Sanjay Patel
  a only has one sibling.
  b is not yet forty.
  c is Scottish.
  d has previous experience in his field.
  e worked in Chicago for two years.

2 Partick is
  a an area in Glasgow.
  b in Scotland.
  c a business centre.
  d a centre for computer technology.
  e where Patel grew up.
  f where Patel is based.

Part 3:   Exam practice

Exam tip: When deciding between the answers to multiple choice questions, do not be misled by answers that look similar to what you have read in the text. For example, there is a difference between 'experts agree' (= all experts agree) and 'some experts say' (= not all experts agree, just some).

Look at the passage below. For each question choose one answer from the letters A–D.

1 Complex information

    A can only be communicated by human beings.

    B is described as intelligent, self-aware and based on context.

    C is communication across species.

    D is too difficult for Campbell's monkeys to understand properly.

2 Chimpanzees

    A are not as intelligent as birds.

    B can be taught language.

    C can play the keyboard.

    D have the language skills of a four-year old child.

3 Birds have shown evidence of being able to

    A teach themselves to solve problems.

    B use multiple tools better than humans do.

    C read numbers as well as people do.

    D sleep better after taking tests.

A scientist based in Scotland claims to have found the first evidence of a common language shared by different animal species. The calls, which are understood by monkeys and birds, were discovered by Klaus Zuberbühler, a psychologist at St Andrews University. According to Zuberbühler, animals and birds can communicate complex ideas not just to their peers but across species.

The findings have been heralded as a significant breakthrough in the quest to discover the origins of human language and proof that the ability to construct a complex form of communication is not unique to man. Zuberbühler made the discovery after spending months observing the calls of Diana monkeys in the Tai Forest in Ivory Coast, in West Africa. He and his colleagues recorded thousands of monkey calls and spent hundreds of hours listening to the animals' noises. They noticed that the monkeys adapted their calls to change the meaning to warn one another about different threats or opportunities. For example, the sight of a leopard prompted a 'krack' alarm call. However, when they merely repeated calls made by other monkeys they added an 'oo'.

The researchers found that the calls could be understood by other species of monkey as well as by some birds. 'What our discovery showed is that the alarm calls were far more complex than we had thought,' said Zuberbühler. 'They were conveying information that was contextual, self-aware and intelligent. We then tried playing these calls back to other monkeys and they responded in ways that showed they knew the meaning. What's more, the same calls would be recognised by other species, like Campbell's monkeys. So they are communicating across species. And since then we have found that hornbill birds can understand these calls and they too can understand all the different meanings.'

Among scientists, the idea that animals and birds might be sentient has been around a long time. Chimpanzees are perhaps the most obvious species for comparisons with humans, but their abilities can still surprise, as when researchers at Georgia State University's language research centre in Atlanta taught some to 'speak'. They taught the animals to use voice synthesisers and a keyboard to hold conversations with humans. One chimp developed a 3,000-word vocabulary and tests suggested she had the language and cognitive skills of a four-year-old child.

Perhaps the most surprising signs of intelligence have been found in birds – whose tiny heads and small brains were long assumed to be a complete barrier to sentience. All that is changing fast, however, with many species showing powerful memories and reasoning power. A few years ago Irene Pepperberg of the Massachusetts Institute of Technology taught a parrot to recognise and count up to six objects and describe their shapes.

Last year that was topped by Alex Kacelnik, a professor of behavioural ecology at Oxford, who discovered that crows are capable of using multiple tools in complex sequences, the first time such behaviour had been observed in non-humans. In an experiment seven crows successfully reeled in a piece of food placed out of reach using three different lengths of stick. Crucially, they were able to complete the task without any special training, suggesting the birds were capable of a level of abstract reasoning and creativity normally associated only with humans.

Last week it emerged that researchers from Padua University in Italy had found that birds were able to read numbers from left to right, as humans do, and count to four even when the line of numbers was moved from vertical to horizontal. They also showed that birds performed better in tests after a good night's sleep.

All this is powerful evidence against the idea that people are unique.

Glossary:
species: a class of plants or animals whose members have the same main characteristics and are able to breed with each other
peer: (here) members of the same species
sentient: capable of experiencing things through its senses

6 Scientists at work

Exam focus: Completing sentences and diagram labels

Aims: Understanding the meaning of words | Skim-reading to find information
Representing information visually | Recognising paraphrase

Part 1: Vocabulary

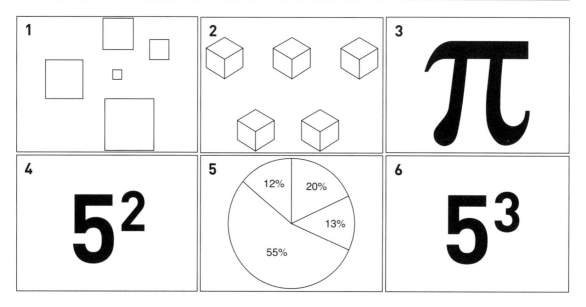

1 Match the pictures 1–6 above with the words a–f.

a pi _____
b a pie chart _____

c 5 cubed _____
d 5 cubes _____

e 5 squared _____
f 5 squares _____

2 Draw a table like the one below and put these words into the correct group, depending on the word ending.

acoustics
anatomy
astronomy
ballistics
biology
botany
cartography
chemistry
computing

ecology
economics
electronics
engineering
genetics
geography
geology
geometry
mathematics

mechanics
meteorology
optometry
palaeontology
pharmacology
physics
statistics
zoology

-logy	-metry	-graphy	-ics	-ing	other

3 Many scientific terms are made up of parts that derive from Greek. Knowing the meaning of the parts of a word can help you understand the meaning of the word as a whole.

Look at the table below which gives the meaning of some Greek word parts. Then match the words 1–12 with the definitions a–l.

Greek word or word part	Meaning	Greek word or word part	Meaning
ana	up	-nomy	the arranging of
astron	star	oikos	house or home
bios	life	palaios	old
botanikos	of herbs (plants)	pharmakon	medicine or drug
ge	the earth or land	physis	nature
-graphy	the writing or drawing of	tomia	cutting
-logy	the science or study of	zoo	animal
-meteoron	of the atmosphere		
-metry	the measuring of		

1 anatomy _____
a the scientific study of animals

2 astronomy _____
b the branch of medicine concerned with the bodily structure of living beings, as revealed by the separation of parts

3 biology _____
c the branch of science concerned with fossils (= the remains of prehistoric plants or animals embedded in rock)

4 botany _____
d the branch of science which deals with stars, space, etc.

5 ecology _____
e the branch of medicine concerned with the uses and effect of drugs

6 geometry _____
f the branch of biology that deals with the relations of organisms to one another and to their physical surroundings

7 palaeontology _____
g the scientific study of plants

8 pharmacology _____
h the branch of mathematics concerned with the properties and relations of point, lines, solids, etc.

9 physics _____
i the study of living organisms

10 meteorology _____
j the branch of science concerned with the atmosphere, especially as a means to forecasting the weather

11 geology _____
k the science which deals with the physical structure and substance of the earth

12 zoology _____
l the branch of science concerned with the nature and properties of matter and energy

4 Which of the subjects in Exercise 2 have you studied yourself?

5 The words 1–5 below are from Exercise 2. Match the words with the fields of study they relate to a–e.

Use a dictionary if you want to.

1	acoustics _____	a	maps
2	ballistics _____	b	circuits (closed systems that electric current can flow around)
3	cartography _____	c	motion (movement)
4	electronics _____	d	sound
5	mechanics _____	e	bullets and guns

6 The noun for a person who practises a particular science or art often ends in *-er* or *-ist*. What do you call a person who ...

Use a dictionary if you want to.

1 draws maps? _____
2 studies biology? _____
3 studies genetics? _____
4 studies plants? _____
5 studies physics? _____

6 studies palaeontology? _____
7 studies ecology? _____
8 studies astronomy? _____
9 studies geology? _____

7 In the following text, underline:

a words related to scientific study, activity or topics
b words related to scientific equipment

Use your dictionary if necessary.

Last month the Institute of Cell and Molecular Science (ICMS) was opened, giving an insight into the traditionally secret world of the scientist.

When the project was being planned, classes of schoolchildren were asked to describe how they saw scientists. They all gave details of white middle-aged men with glasses and beards. Only one girl chose to describe a female scientist, but even she had a beard. When the children were asked about cells, they thought of prison cells, even battery cells, but never the cells that make up all of us.

Visiting schoolchildren will be able to watch scientists at work among the test tubes, flasks, microscopes and centrifuges of a state-of-the-art research facility. They can then enter The Centre of the Cell – the 'embryo' pod – where they can learn about the basics of cell biology, disease and genetics. After seeing the scientists at work, children enter the pod where interactive screens will give them a theatrical taste of everything from cell division and tooth decay to cancer, cloning and gene therapy.

8 Find words in the text in Exercise 7 that collocate with the words 1–5. To help you, the definitions of the words you are looking for are given in brackets.

1 _____ an insight (offering)

2 _____ details (provided)

3 _____ equipment (the best available because it has been made using the most modern techniques and technology)

4 tooth _____ (the state or process of being gradually destroyed by a natural process)

5 gene _____ (the treatment of illness without the use of drugs or operations)

Part 2: Practice exercises

 Exam information: Completion tasks (2)
Completion tasks assess your ability to find and understand detailed or specific information in a text.

- **Completing a diagram or picture**
  You will be asked to read a description in a passage and use words from it to complete labels on a diagram or picture.
  The answers will often come from the same part of the text, but may not be in the same order as the questions.

- **Completing sentences**
  You will be asked to complete sentences with words from a passage.
  The answers will be in the same order as the questions: you should be able to find the answer to question 1 before the answer to question 2, and so on.

In both types of task you will be told how many words to use, e.g. NO MORE THAN TWO WORDS, ONE WORD ONLY, NO MORE THAN TWO WORDS AND A NUMBER, NO MORE THAN THREE WORDS OR NUMBERS.

- If you use more words, you will not get a mark.
- Numbers can be written in numbers (e.g. *5*) or words (e.g. *five*).
- Hyphenated words count as one word (e.g. *state-of-the-art* counts as one word).

1 Skim-read the passage and find the sections that refer to:
a size, weight or other physical properties of brains
b intelligence

Dolphins have been declared the world's second most intelligent creatures after humans, with scientists suggesting they are so bright that they should be treated as 'non-human persons'.
  Studies into dolphin behaviour have highlighted how similar their communications are to those of humans and that they are brighter than chimpanzees. These have been backed up by anatomical research showing that dolphin brains have many key features associated with high intelligence. The researchers argue that their work shows it is morally unacceptable to keep such intelligent animals in amusement parks or to kill them for food or by accident when fishing. Some 300,000 whales, dolphins and porpoises die in this way each year.
  'Many dolphin brains are larger than our own and second in mass only to the human brain when corrected for body size,' said Lori Marino, a zoologist at Emory University in Atlanta,

Georgia, who has used magnetic resonance imaging scans to map the brains of dolphin species and compare them with those of primates. 'The neuroanatomy suggests psychological continuity between humans and dolphins and has profound implications for the ethics of human-dolphin interactions,' she added.

Dolphins have long been recognised as among the most intelligent of animals. Recently, a series of behavioural studies has suggested that dolphins, especially species such as the bottlenose, whose brains weigh about 5lb, could even be brighter than chimps, which some studies have found can reach the intelligence levels of three-year-old children. The studies show how dolphins have distinct personalities, a strong sense of self and can think about the future.

It has also become clear that they are 'cultural' animals, meaning that new types of behaviour can quickly be picked up by one dolphin from another. In one study, Diana Reiss, professor of psychology at Hunter College, City University of New York, showed that bottlenose dolphins could recognise themselves in a mirror and use it to inspect various parts of their bodies, an ability that had been thought limited to humans and great apes. In another, she found that captive animals also had the ability to learn a rudimentary symbol-based language.

Other research has shown dolphins can solve difficult problems, while those living in the wild co-operate in ways that imply complex social structures and a high level of emotional sophistication. In one recent case, a dolphin rescued from the wild was taught to tail-walk while recuperating for three weeks in a dolphinarium in Australia. After she was released, scientists were astonished to see the trick spreading among wild dolphins who had learnt it from the former captive. There are many similar examples, such as the way dolphins living off Western Australia learnt to hold sponges over their snouts to protect themselves when searching for spiny fish on the ocean floor. Such observations, along with others showing, for example, how dolphins could co-operate with military precision to round up shoals of fish to eat, have prompted questions about the brain structures that must underlie them.

Size is only one factor. Researchers have found that brain size varies hugely from around 7oz for smaller cetacean species such as the Ganges River dolphin to more than 19lb for sperm whales, whose brains are the largest on the planet. Human brains, by contrast, range from 2lb–4lb, while a chimp's brain is about 12oz. When it comes to intelligence, however, brain size is less important than its size relative to the body. What Marino and her colleagues found was that the cerebral cortex and neocortex of bottlenose dolphins were so large that 'the anatomical ratios that assess cognitive capacity place it second only to the human brain'. They also found that the brain cortex of dolphins such as the bottlenose had the same convoluted folds that are strongly linked with human intelligence. Such folds increase the volume of the cortex and the ability of brain cells to interconnect with each other. 'Despite evolving along a different neuroanatomical trajectory to humans, cetacean brains have several features that are correlated with complex intelligence,' Marino said.

'Marino and Reiss will present their findings at a conference in San Diego, California, next month, concluding that the new evidence about dolphin intelligence makes it morally repugnant to mistreat them. Thomas White, professor of ethics at Loyola Marymount University, Los Angeles, who has written a series of academic studies suggesting dolphins should have rights, will speak at the same conference. 'The scientific research . . . suggests that dolphins are "non-human persons" who qualify for moral standing as individuals,' he said.

Glossary

oz: an ounce in weight (1oz = 28g)

lb: a pound in weight (1lb = 454g = 16oz)

> **Exam tip:** When you read texts, think about how you would represent information in a visual way.

2   Use the text on pages 53–54 to complete the diagrams below.

Diagram 1: Brain size

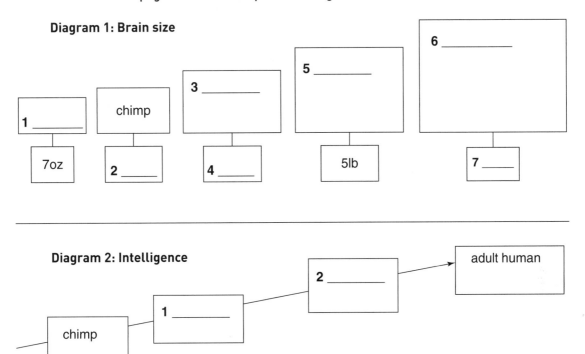

Diagram 2: Intelligence

3   The phrases a–e are from the passage in Exercise 1. Match the sentence beginnings 1–5 with the words a–e. The resulting sentences give information in the same order as the information in the passage.

1 There are reasons to believe that dolphins deserve to be regarded as _____	a morally unacceptable.
2 One of the consequences of this is that using them for entertainment, as we do now, would be _____	b brain structures.
3 In order compare dolphin and human brains, scientists have used _____	c non-human persons.
4 The way dolphins can cooperate and their levels of problem solving have made scientists think again about dolphins' _____	d brain cortex.
5 Scientists have also observed that the intelligence of certain dolphins is suggested by the physical structure of their _____	e imaging scans.

4 Complete the sentences 1–5 using no more than three words from the passage below. The answers follow the order of the questions. Remember to look for paraphrases in the text.

1 Jane Goodall has attained global recognition as a role model for _____.
2 Her studies have had far-reaching consequences, one of them being that we might have to accept that some animals should be treated _____.
3 Goodall believed that the main reason why women made good field scientists was their natural capacity _____.
4 _____ have been encouraged to become field scientists by the example of the three sisters in science.
5 Even today, when women are more visible in the field of science, their role is limited and they do not tend to be the _____.

It is 50 years since Jane Goodall first dipped her toes in the waters of Lake Tanganyika, in what is now the Gombe National Park in Tanzania. Since then she has been responsible for the most comprehensive study of wild chimpanzees – and become an idol of contemporary women scientists around the world.

In 1962, at a time when no woman in the world held a PhD in primatology, Goodall started a PhD in ethology – the scientific study of animal behaviour – at the University of Cambridge. Her resulting thesis, *Nest Building Behaviour in the Free Ranging Chimpanzee*, included the observations that chimps use tools and eat meat. Goodall had redefined our understanding of the origins of Man. Louis Leakey, the famous palaeontologist and Goodall's mentor, said of her work: 'Now we must redefine "tool", redefine "Man", or accept chimpanzees as humans.' Goodall's work, and that of two other female pioneers in primatology, Dian Fossey and Biruté Galdikas, was made possible by the example of Leakey. Born to British missionaries in Kenya in 1903, he was the first white baby the Kikuyu people had seen and he spoke their language before he learnt English. He grew up to be an ardent palaeontologist, archaeologist and anthropologist at the University of Cambridge and, later, with his wife Mary Douglas Nicol.

Leakey thought that the attributes that made a good field scientist were innate to women. Because women were pre-programmed to be mothers, he thought, they had three crucial traits: they were patient, they were better able to understand an animal's desires by observing social non-verbal cues and they were less aggressive than men – all beliefs later echoed by Goodall. He also felt that men were more concerned with conquering nature than committing themselves to detailed field studies.

Goodall's career began in the late 1950s, when she worked as secretary to Leakey at the Coryndon Museum in Nairobi, of which he was the director. In 1960, after the 26-year-old Goodall had assisted on a fossil dig at Olduvai Gorge in Tanzania, she was sent by her mentor to study chimpanzees in the wild. At the insistence of the British Government she arrived in Gombe with her mother, Vanne, in tow. Spending day after day among the primates, she became fascinated by their behaviour and began informal studies. But at the insistence of Leakey, who warned that she would need to formalise her work to gain scientific credibility, she applied for a place at Cambridge.

Since then Goodall and her two sisters in science, Fossey and Galdikas, have paved the way in primatology, a field that is now dominated by women. Gombe is one of the longest running research studies of wild animals anywhere in the world: it has produced 35 PhD theses, more than 30 books and 200 research papers and nine films. Furthermore, according to Julie Des Jardins, the author of *The Madame Curie Complex: the Hidden History of Women in Science*, 78 per cent of all PhDs awarded in primatology in 2000 were awarded to women. Goodall, Fossey and Galdikas have helped to inspire generations of women to pick up their binoculars and take to the world's fields and forests.

Goodall comes from a dynasty of strong women and describes her mother and grandmother as 'those two amazing, strong women, undaunted'. Goodall's mother did not laugh at her daughter when she said she was going to Africa. 'My mother used to say: "If you really want something and you work hard and never give up, you find a way",' Goodall says. "She was definitely the greatest inspiration that I had.'

If only science's old guard had had the same attitude. Today's scientific community was formalised by men. As a consequence of the scientific 'revolution' of the 17th and 18th centuries, science moved from the home to laboratories, universities and hospitals, establishments to which women were denied access, irrespective of their aptitude or contribution. In most fields of scientific research, most of the big players continue to be men. According to the UKRC (the body responsible for advancing gender equality in science, engineering and technology), in the 2007–08 academic year, in STEM – science, technology, engineering and maths – subjects, about one third of researchers were women. But in the higher reaches of the academic world, the numbers fall away. About a quarter of lecturers and fewer than one in ten professors are female.

Perhaps this under-representation of women in science has in part been caused by a lack of prominent role models. The women who flourished under the guidance of Leakey, however, provide ample proof that if women are given opportunities, they can surpass all expectation. They can tread their own path through the forest and conduct credible research with far-reaching and long-lasting implications.

Jane Goodall still believes that her mother's words about working hard to achieve a goal have the power to inspire young women who dream of becoming scientists. 'I would say to them what Mum said to me,' she says. Clearly, it works.

Part 3: Exam practice

Using NO MORE THAN THREE WORDS from the passage, complete each gap in the diagram below.

Holidaymakers faced disruption yesterday because of new plumes of ash from an Icelandic volcano, which forced the closure of airports in Spain and Portugal.

The cancellations – which mainly affected Ryanair and easyJet services operating out of Stansted and Gatwick – came as scientists produced the first internal map of Eyjafjallajokull's network of magma chambers, which extend 12 miles below the ground.

A new ash cloud has risen 30,000ft into the air and drifted south after a pulse of meltwater and ice poured into the Eyjafjallajokull volcano last week. The water caused huge explosions as it hit the hot lava, generating more ash plumes. European aviation regulators have imposed a maximum safe limit of 0.002 grammes of ash per cubic metre of air, meaning that if levels rise above this, flights cannot enter that airspace.

The map shows how the volcano's tubes plunge deep down through the earth's crust to the start of the mantle, which is made of semi-molten rock. It reveals the huge scale of the eruption and the potential for a far greater one. This is because the magma chamber of Eyjafjallajokull is dwarfed by the much larger one under Katla, a volcano 15 miles to the east. Two of Katla's eruptions, in 1612 and 1821, are thought to have been triggered by those of its neighbour. While Katla is not part of the same underground network of magma channels and chambers, it is close enough to be affected by changes in pressure in Eyjafjallajokull's system. There is also a chance that a horizontal sheet of magma, known as a dike, beneath Eyjafjallajokull could stretch out far enough to penetrate a magma chamber beneath Katla. Hitting the roots of its neighbour would almost certainly trigger an eruption. The three eruptions of Eyjafjallajokull on record have each been associated with a subsequent eruption of Katla. There have, so far, been no signs of turbulence beneath Katla's surface but, having last erupted in 1918, vulcanologists say that a new blast is overdue.

The workings of the volcanoes have been provisionally drawn up by Professor Erik Sturkell, a geologist at the Nordic Volcanological Centre, University of Iceland. Sturkell suggests the Eyjafjallajokull eruption has been building since 1994, when new lava began rising, forming two reservoirs three miles beneath the volcano. A surge of earthquakes under Katla mean it has experienced a similar influx of lava, Sturkell said. 'This suggests the volcano is close to eruption.'

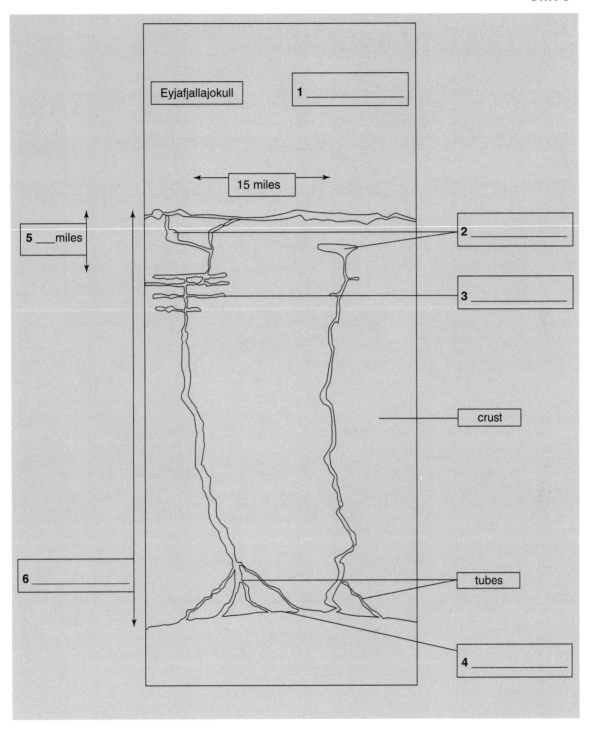

Eyjafjallajokull

1 _____

15 miles

5 ___miles

2 _____

3 _____

crust

6 _____

tubes

4 _____

7 The job market

Part 1: Vocabulary

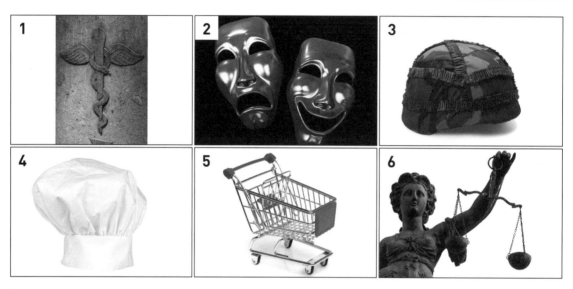

1 Match the pictures 1–6 above with the careers a–f they symbolise.

a acting _____   c medicine _____   e the army _____
b catering _____   d retail _____   f the law _____

2 Match the job sectors and industries 1–6 with the definitions a–f.

1 hospitality _____	a the way shops and businesses organise the sale of their products, for example the way they are displayed and the prices that are chosen
2 merchandising _____	b the business of selling houses, buildings, and land
3 recruitment _____	c the business of giving expert advice on a particular subject to a company or organization
4 real estate _____	d the business of providing food, drink, and other privileges for visitors or clients at major sporting or other public events
5 consultancy _____	e the business of building things such as houses, factories, roads, and bridges
6 construction _____	f the process of selecting people for an organisation and persuading them to join

3 Underline at least ten words or phrases related to the topic of work in the passage below. Use your dictionary if necessary.

Universities are expanding opportunities to spend a year overseas, meaning that not only language students benefit from time spent in another culture. Amanda Harper, head of placements at Bath University, says going abroad offers students the chance to widen their cultural horizons and develop an international network of friends and contacts.

'One of my science students learnt to dance salsa and speak Spanish during his year in Costa Rica,' she says. 'The students mature and their confidence increases. These changes are unquantifiable in terms of marks but the time management skills, presentation skills and ability to deal with the world are vastly improved when they come back from their placements.'

As it becomes increasingly difficult to stand out in the graduate job market, a year's experience in another country could be what separates one student from others with the same results. A survey for the Confederation of British Industry found that 56 per cent of employers were not satisfied with graduates' foreign language skills and 40 per cent were dissatisfied with candidates' international cultural awareness.

Most overseas placements are taken in the third year of university, after which students return for a fourth and final year. Cassandra Popli, 22, who spent a year at California State University in Long Beach, got a job in California which she will take up after graduating from Swansea University this summer. 'I feel like I have got so much more from that year abroad than I would have if I had stayed here,' she adds.

4 In the text from Exercise 3, find words that collocate with the words 1–6.

1 expand _____
2 go _____
3 widen _____
4 _____ a network
5 increase _____
6 take up a _____

5 Complete the passage with the words a–k.

a counterparts
b gap
c industries
d ladder
e managers
f market
g rate
h recession
i salaries
j study
k workforce

Young women entering the current job (1) _____ have more than fifty years to wait before they could be paid the same as men. Female managers saw their pay increase half a percentage point faster than their male counterparts last year, according to a (2) _____ by the Chartered Management Institute. Even if that (3) _____ of improvement continues, the pay (4) _____ will not be closed until 2067.

Women's (5) _____ increased by 2.8 per cent in 2009, compared with 2.3 per cent for men. There is better news in the boardroom, however, where female (6) _____ out-earn men with an average salary of £144,729 compared with £138,765. At the other end of the career (7) _____ , junior male executives receive £22,253 on average – £1,065 more than their female (8) _____ .

The largest pay gaps were in the IT and pharmaceutical (9) _____, at £17,736 and £14,018 respectively. The Midlands has the worst regional divide.

The (10) _____ also appears to have hit women managers hard, with 4.5 per cent of the female (11) _____ made redundant last year, compared with three per cent of men.

The general secretary of the trade union Unison, said: 'It is a disgrace that women will have to wait until 2067 for the pay gap to close – nearly 100 years after the Equal Pay Act. This glacial progress towards fairness cannot be allowed to go on.'

6 Match the statements 1–15 with statements a–o.

1 I work with animals. ____	a I am having cash flow problems.
2 I am buying baby clothes today. ____	b I am an actor.
3 I administer first aid. ____	c I am applying for jobs.
4 I solve computer problems. ____	d I work in IT.
5 I will get redundancy pay. ____	e I do a lot of voice-overs.
6 I deliver babies. ____	f I am on strike.
7 I have appeared in several commercials. ____	g I am getting a pay rise.
8 You can hear my voice in a commercial. ____	h I am on maternity leave.
9 I am filling in forms and updating my CV. ____	i I am retiring.
10 My job is taking care of my family. ____	j I am being laid off.
11 My wages will increase by seven per cent. ____	k I am a paramedic.
12 My products are selling well, but I am having problems paying my bills at the moment. ____	l I work as a midwife.
13 I present a radio programme. ____	m I am a veterinarian.
14 I am unhappy with my working conditions and am doing something about it. ____	n I work in broadcasting.
15 I will soon be collecting my pension. ____	o I am a househusband.

7 Answer the questions 1–5. Use a dictionary if necessary.

1 Can you list all the jobs you and people in your family have had?

2 What industries were these jobs in?

3 Which professions or industries would you never consider working in?

4 Which of these are more important to you: type of work, pay, colleagues or working conditions?

5 Blue-collar workers usually have manual jobs, whereas white-collar workers usually work in an office. Who is likely to get wages? Who is likely to get a salary?

6 Name three jobs that a blue-collar worker might do. Name three jobs that a white-collar worker might do.

8 Unscramble the anagrams 1–12. They are all words from Exercises 1–7.

1 sweag _____
2 crowefork _____
3 talier _____
4 trenkow _____
5 dunystir _____
6 tutinccosonr _____
7 youcanclstn _____
8 penelmact _____
9 partnertouc _____
10 ginshandcremi _____
11 gnitsacdaorb _____
12 vtrnrneieiaa _____

> **Exam tip:** Vocabulary cannot be learnt without revision. Try to revise little and often.

Part 2: Practice exercises

 Exam information: Completing notes, summaries, or flow charts

This task tests your ability to understand the main ideas in a section of text or to understand details.

You are given a summary of information from a text, but there will be information missing which you have to find in the text. The summary may consist of connected sentences of text or a flow chart, which is a series of steps linked by arrows to show a sequence of events.

The answers are unlikely to be in the same order as you will find them in the text, but you usually only have to look at a section of text, not the whole.

You have to select a certain number of words (e.g. one, two or three) from the text or choose the right word from a list of possible answers.

Exam tip: When you are completing notes or a summary, try to predict what kinds of words may be missing by using your knowledge of grammar.

1   Draw a table like the one below and put the words into the correct group. Some words belong in more than one group.

additional   business   calculated   consumer   economic   employ   harmful   job
management   market   maximise   offer   product   search   value

Verbs	Nouns	Adjectives

2   Read the passage. Predict what type of word is missing in the spaces 1–8 and give an example of a possible answer. The first one has been done for you.

> Jobs drive demand in the economy and they drive consumer and (1) _____ confidence. A jobless recovery, or worse, a job-loss recovery, is of little (2) _____ .
>
> The recent economic numbers have been (3) _____, including that highly encouraging 0.8% for third-quarter gross domestic product (GDP) growth and last week's better-than-expected purchasing managers' surveys for manufacturing and services.
>
> Numbers are numbers, jobs are real. Most people do not spend time poring over the national accounts or (4) _____ . Economic misery or joy is (5) _____ defined by the state of the labour market.
>
> What counts, therefore, is whether growth is (6) _____ into employment. Friday's better American job numbers have not altered a picture in (7) _____ unemployment hangs like a cloud over America. The state of the job market helps to explain why America appears more (8) _____ and depressed by the downturn than many other countries, including Britain.

1   noun: 'and' is a coordinating conjunction and we would expect the same type of structure before and after it. 'Consumer' is a noun used as an adjective before 'confidence'.

Possible answer: retail

3 Below are three options for each of the spaces 1–8 in the passage in Exercise 2 on page 64. Use the predictions you made in Exercise 2 and choose the best option for the context.

	a	**b**	**c**
1	business	shoppers	raise
2	spending	jobs	use
3	good	down	calculate
4	accountant	international	surveys
5	mainly	rarely	last
6	found	converted	mostly
7	which	America's	whose
8	encouraged	poverty	damaged

> **Exam tip:** Always follow the exam instructions carefully, or you will lose marks.
> In tasks that ask you to summarise, the following instructions apply:
> • You are told how many words you can use in your answer.
> • Numbers can be written using figures or words. A number or symbol counts as one word.
> • Hyphenated words count as single words.

4 Look at the answers 1–5 which were given by a student. The instructions were to use 'NO MORE THAN THREE WORDS' from the text. For which answer(s) will she not get a mark?

1 the downturn
2 for manufacturing & services
3 the job-loss recovery
4 the jobless recovery
5 0.8 per cent growth

> **Exam tip:** Summaries are usually based on a specific section of the text, so do not waste your time reading sections you do not need to complete the task.

5 Read the (incomplete) summary and state briefly what it is about.

> Students who work need to make sure that they are not being taken advantage of. If they are aware of (1) _____, they can ensure that their employers treat them fairly. If they are (2) _____ than twenty-one years old, they should be earning just under £6.00 per hour. The law is also clear about the right to certain breaks and to a (3) _____. However, agency workers have fewer rights than (4) _____. Student workers also have responsibilities, for example, they have to pay (5) _____.

6 Scan the passage and find the section that relates to the topic of the summary in Exercise 5 above.

> The current graduate job market is the toughest in recent memory. The traditional recruiters are taking on fewer graduates, and the class of 2010 are, in many cases, competing with the class of 2009 for those posts available. But the difficulties for students do not end there: for those either starting or returning to a course this autumn, the market for part-time work is just as tough.

For the majority of full-time undergraduates, part-time employment is a vital source of supplementary income. Most studies show that at least 50 per cent of students work during term time, and around 90 per cent in vacations. About 70 per cent of those in work say that they do so to cover basic living expenses, so this is not just to fund socialising either.

It seems likely, however, that the current cohort of students may find it more difficult than their predecessors to find such employment. There are fewer jobs to find, and much greater competition from the non-student population for those that still exist – recent estimates put the number of people in part-time employment at record levels, as fewer full-time posts are available in the general economy.

But if you are a student looking for additional income, there are steps that you can take to maximise your chances of getting a job. Most universities will have a job shop, operated by the institution or the students' union. As these cater specifically for students, they will at least make the search easier. In addition, most if not all will, to some extent, filter the jobs to ensure that the employers are not completely evil, and will offer help with key job application skills such as writing CVs, personal statements and interview techniques. You can find a list at www.nases.org.uk.

Students' unions themselves often employ large numbers of student staff, usually with relatively good pay and conditions. The trick here is to apply well before term starts, as any jobs are usually gone by freshers' week (not least because the staff need to be in place by then).

If you do not like the idea of a boss, you could also consider self-employment. For example, if you have particular skills, such as design or computer programming, you can advertise these on sites such as Student Gems (www.studentgems.com).

For those of you who do find work, there are also various points to keep in mind. The National Union of Students is often asked to put a figure on the maximum hours that a student should work. There are a range of opinions on this: often the figure of 16 hours a week is mentioned, whereas Cambridge University forbids its students from taking up employment during term time. Of course, what is suitable for you will depend on your circumstances – a history student with ten hours of formal classes a week might be able to work more than a medicine student with 35.

Research has shown that there is a correlation between a high number of hours worked and the likelihood you will end up with a lower degree classification, so you should be careful about balancing any work with your studies. You might also want to consider when you work: night shifts might pay better but they can have a harmful effect on your coursework.

Then there is the issue of what sort of work. In an ideal world, students would be able to find employment in areas that are relevant to their future careers, or at least which pay well. Alas, this was never easy, and may well be all the more difficult now. In any case, most students are still to be found in low-paid and low-skilled jobs in catering and retail.

But whether you are bar staff or an agency nurse, you need to know your rights. Employers have to obey the law, no matter how challenging the job market is. For example, you should be paid at least the minimum wage – from October it is £4.92 an hour if you are 18–21 or £5.93 an hour if you are older. All employees are entitled to a written contract, and a rest period if your shift is six hours or longer. Part-time employees cannot be treated less favourably than full-time workers, although if you work through an agency, you can be treated less favourably at present than permanent employees in certain circumstances, so be careful. A full list of rights is available at www.direct.gov.uk/employees.

One way to ensure that your rights are upheld is to join a trade union. They can help you discuss employment matters with your bosses and bargain for better rights in your workplace. Student workers often get a rough deal – but there is safety in numbers.

Talking of numbers, one last thing to watch out for is tax. Students are actually liable for income tax, contrary to popular belief. Fear not, though, as at present 80 per cent of students don't earn above their 'personal allowance' (the amount everyone can earn before tax is applied, which is £6,475 in 2010/11, rising to £7,475 in 2011/12). However, because of their erratic work patterns, and the way tax is calculated, students can sometimes end up paying tax erroneously – so if you think you have, contact HM Revenue and Customs about a refund – www.hmrc.gov.uk/incometax.

7 Complete the summary in Exercise 5 using **NO MORE THAN TWO WORDS** taken from the text for each gap. Refer only to the relevant part of the text.

8 Find the section of the text in Exercise 6 that is relevant to the flow chart below. Then complete the flow chart using **NO MORE THAN TWO WORDS** from the text for each gap.

HOW TO LOOK FOR WORK WHILE YOU STUDY

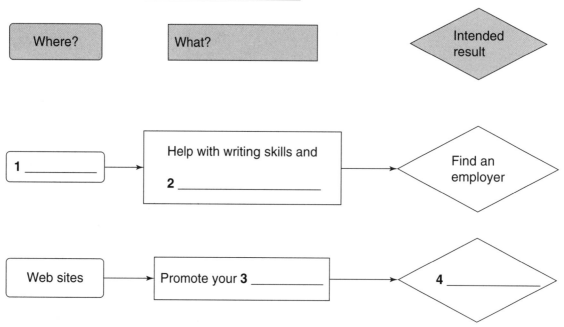

Where?   What?   Intended result

1 _____ → Help with writing skills and 2 _____ → Find an employer

Web sites → Promote your 3 _____ → 4 _____

Part 3: Exam practice

Complete the summary below with words from the text underneath. Use NO MORE THAN THREE WORDS for each answer.

Summary:

Up until recently, students expected to earn good money after graduation. However, there has been a dramatic (1) _____ in attitude, and a minority now think that they will work in a field that they are (2) _____ for. It is still worth doing higher studies in the UK because the gap in earning between university graduates and the people who do not have university degrees is greater than anywhere else (3) _____. Because of the current economic situation, there may be fewer employment opportunities available, so for (4) _____, qualifications are very important.

The recession has brought about an abrupt change of mood on university campuses up and down the country. A five-year boom in the graduate job market has been stopped in its tracks and salary expectations, which hit record levels last year, are heading southwards. No wonder only one in five of 16,000 final year students questioned for a recent survey by High Flyers Research said that they expected to get a job for which they are qualified by the time they graduate this summer.

Despite the gloom, the financial case for going to university remains compelling. International surveys continue to show the salary premium enjoyed by UK graduates over those who choose not to go to university as among the highest in the world. In the post-recession world, a university degree is likely to be even more of an advantage to job-seekers than before.

But choosing the right degree course and the right university will also be more important than ever. This does not necessarily mean that students should go only for job-related degrees, but it will put a premium on marketable skills. And it may mean that more universities can be expected to follow the lead of Liverpool John Moores University, which puts all of its undergraduates through a World of Work (WoW) course designed to give them the problem-solving and communications skills they will need at work.

The Times Good University Guide 2010, published by HarperCollins, offers a wealth of essential information to help candidates to navigate the maze of university choice, as well as advice on student life. It is the most authoritative guide to universities in the UK and is an essential and comprehensive tool for students and parents.

The online version of the Guide allows students and parents to create their own individual university rankings and to compare the strengths and weaknesses of different institutions by sorting universities according to one of eight criteria – from student satisfaction to research quality and degree results. The table sees Oxford maintain its leadership, despite coming below Cambridge in most of the subject tables. Cambridge has the better record on student satisfaction, research, entry standards, completion and graduate destinations, but Oxford's lead in staffing levels, degree classifications and particularly in spending on libraries and other student facilities makes the difference.

The biggest climbers at the top of the table include Liverpool (up from 43 to 28), Leeds (up from 31 to 27), Sheffield (up from 22 to 18), Edinburgh (up from 18 to 14) and Exeter (up from 13 to nine). St Andrews remains the top university in Scotland, while Cardiff is well clear in Wales.

The key information is contained in the 62 subject tables, which now cover every area of higher education. The number of institutions in this year's tables has increased by only one because a fourth university – the West of Scotland – has instructed the Higher Education Statistics Agency not to release its data. It joins Swansea Metropolitan, London Metropolitan and Liverpool Hope universities in blocking the release of data to avoid appearing in league tables.

8 Twenty-somethings

Part 1: Vocabulary

1   The topic of this unit is 'twenty-somethings'. This refers to young people who are in their twenties, i.e. between twenty and thirty years old. The words a–f below also refer to numbers.

Match the pictures 1–6 above with the words a–f.

a   a couple _____   d   a quartet _____
b   a dozen _____   e   triplets _____
c   a pair _____   f   twelve-ish _____

2   Work out the meaning of the words in italics in by studying their context in the sentences 1–4.

1   More twenty-somethings want to be homeowners than ever before, according to research done on behalf of the Council of *Mortgage* Lenders (CML).

a   a small sum of money
b   a type of property
c   a loan for a house

2   The CML has asked young people the same questions about home-ownership *aspirations* periodically since 1975.

a   belongings
b   desires
c   age groups

3 As term time starts, students are being warned by Shelter, the housing charity, to beware of *scams* involving privately-rented property.

   a tricks to get somebody's money
   b types of student accommodation
   c surveys about attitudes

4 Two million people in Great Britain know someone who has either lost money or had problems *retrieving* their deposit.

   a getting back
   b asking for
   c paying first

> **Exam tip:** To better understand opinions expressed in texts, think about the writer's word choice. You need to know whether the words that are used have positive or negative connotations.

3 The words and phrases 1–15 are all ways of referring to old people. Do they usually have positive or negative connotations, or are they neutral? Write P (positive), N (negative), or NL (neutral).

1 advanced in years _____

2 ancient _____

3 decrepit _____

4 elderly _____

5 getting on _____

6 mature _____

7 not as young as one was _____

8 not long for this world _____

9 octogenarian _____

10 over the hill _____

11 past it _____

12 past one's prime _____

13 senile _____

14 senior _____

15 septuagenarian _____

4 Match words from Exercise 3 above with their definitions a–f.

   a old and weak _____

   b confused and no longer able to remember things or look after yourself because of old age _____

   c a person who is between eighty and eighty-nine years old _____

   d approaching death _____

   e a person who is between seventy and seventy-nine years old _____

   f very old, or having existed for a long time _____

5 Write a paragraph about your family and/or your future, in which you use at least five of the words from Exercise 3.

Part 2: Practice exercises

 Exam information: True / False / Not Given

This type of question tests if you can identify whether information is correct or not.

You are given a factual statement and you have to check in a text if it is true. It is important <u>not</u> to use your own knowledge to answer the questions; the answer must come from the text.

- If the text confirms the statement, your answer should be 'TRUE'.
- If the test says the opposite is true, your answer should be 'FALSE'.
- If it is impossible to know from the text if the statement is true or not, your answer should be 'NOT GIVEN'.

The information in the text will be in the same order as the questions.

Exam tip: As the answers are in the same order as the text, do not waste time going back to the beginning of a text to find the answer to a question. Always keep reading on.

1   Read the text and when one of the topics on the right is mentioned, tick it. One topic is not mentioned at all, but do not re-read the text to find it. It is a good idea always to keep in mind the next <u>two</u> topics. If you find the second one, then the first one is probably not mentioned. Move on to the next topic. If you come to the end of the text and you find there is more than one topic that you have not found, <u>then</u> you can have another look at the text.

For British teenagers and twenty-somethings today, life is increasingly becoming unfair. The world into which they are entering is more testing and uncertain than the one their parents negotiated at the same age. Finding a stable career is harder, home ownership is a pipedream and while higher education may be more accessible, rising student debt – and national debt – is something they will be paying off for years.

It is a scenario that has been seized on by publishers. Ed Howker and Shiv Malik, both 29, have just finished a book completely dedicated to the subject. When they began their book, they assumed that their constricting circumstances were of their own making. 'At first, we were kind of upset with ourselves,' Malik said. 'We thought, it's our fault. We're lazy. We're not working hard enough. But we found ourselves getting increasingly angry, and realised we were justified in feeling that the whole country had forgotten about the young.'

He compared what the Norwegians did with their North Sea Oil revenue (investing it into a £300 billion trust for subsequent generations) to what we did (subsidised tax break binge for a few decades). They said it was not a surprise that so many reached 30 'but don't feel as though they have entered adulthood in any meaningful sense'.

Topics
- debt
- marriage
- guilt
- accommodation
- participation in society

Renting is most common among 25 to 35-year-olds, but the instability of six-month contracts make forming relationships and cohabitation difficult. Malik said that he had moved flat ten times in ten years. He and his wife now live in a house with a friend. They have iPads and world travel (if they save enough), but home ownership or 'a decent job with decent pay' is more unlikely.

Howker admitted that some Baby Boomer parents helped their children financially but this was no use. 'Nothing is going to slow down social mobility more than ensuring young people end up living the lives their parents can afford for them. The last thing this country needs is some kind of battle of the generations. But we need to start thinking seriously about what kind of future we want. And if our generation is going to fix that, we need to be active in our communities and in politics.'

It's a solution that does not seem instant to a problem that does not seem fair. But then, as any parent will tell you, life is not fair.

> **Exam tip:** Try to anticipate what the answer might look like before you search for it in the text. You may find it a lot quicker this way and good timing is essential in a test.

2 **Paraphrase the expressions a–c in as many ways as you can.**

a proportion   **b** unemployed   **c** the highest level

Now look for the answers to the questions 1–3 in the text below.

1 What *proportion* of people under 25 are unemployed at the moment? _____

2 How many people between 16 and 25 are *unemployed*? _____

3 What is *the highest level* of unemployment so far? _____

The increase in youth unemployment, as those with little or no job experience lose out to older workers in increasingly competitive appointment processes, has given rise to concern. More than one in six young people are out of work, raising fears of a 'lost generation' of potential workers.

Official data showed yesterday that in the three months to June, the number of those under 25 and out of work had soared by 50,000, or 6 per cent, to 928,000 as school- and college-leavers have been unable to find jobs. Some 722,000 of these are aged 18 to 24, while the remaining 206,000 are aged 16 to 17.

The jobless rate among the 18–24 age group, at about one in six, is closing in on the all-time high of 17.8 per cent set in March 1993, after the 1990s recession.

Exam tip: Improving your reading speed can also help you with your timing. Work on adapting your speed according to your reading purpose: you can read fast to get the main information, but when you are looking for detail, you may need to read more slowly.

3   **You will need a watch for this exercise.**

The two texts below are of the same word length. They are both about the current trend of thirty-something marriages. In Text 1 the writer argues in favour them, whereas in Text 2 the writer suggests that getting married younger could be better.

Start with Text 1. Make a note of your starting time. Read each paragraph as fast as you can, without stopping for unknown vocabulary, but make sure you try to understand what you read. You can check this each time by answering the (simple) question at the end of each paragraph, first of all without looking back at what you have just read. If you cannot answer this question, you were probably reading too fast and you will have to read the paragraph again to answer the question. If you can answer it correctly, move on to the next paragraph but try to read it a little faster than the one before. Make a note of your finishing time.

Now do the same for Text 2. Check if you managed to complete Text 2 in less time than Text 1.

Text 1

I married in both my twenties and my thirties. I was 28 the first time and my wife was 22. While we're talking about numbers, it's probably worth mentioning that our combined emotional age was about 17. We were both carrying baggage, not from previous relationships but from childhood and adolescence, which meant that we were both still working on our identities. We weren't unusual in this respect; 21st-century Westerners enjoy a protracted adolescence, during which it can be risky to make any 'commitments'.

How many times has the writer been married?

Anyway, we had been together for two years before we blundered into marriage. Our reasons were laudable enough – love, wanting to be together, that kind of thing. What we hadn't done was to talk seriously about what we wanted from life, in terms of kids, careers, where to live, what values to hold dear and so on, probably because we didn't have a clue. About three years into the marriage it became apparent that our views on these matters were diverging. The relationship began to unravel and I was divorced by the age of 33.

Did the author divorce because he and his wife had very different backgrounds?

After a three-year courtship I remarried last month, at 37. When Clara and I met, we both had well established careers, friends, values, wants and tastes. Far from making us inflexible, part of the fun has been exploring each other's substantial worlds. I met Clara's host of interesting friends; she met both of mine. I showed her how to eat oysters; she taught me that some flowers are edible. I was introduced to the wonders of Cornwall; Clara was surprised to find out about my love of musicals. We both had disposable income and our own flats, so our courtship was characterised by great meals out, holidays, lazy Sunday mornings ... it was sophisticated, hedonistic and fun.

True or false: the writer is saying that it is better to get married when both partners have already established their own identities.

Not in a way that left us unprepared for toil and practicality, though. We had our first child a year ago and our life is unrecognisable from that described above, but we love it – and each other – even more, because we were ready and we knew what we wanted. So, for me, unless you are a particularly precocious or self-aware twenty-something, the thirties are a better bet for marriage.

True or false: the writer suggests that his experience is clear evidence that getting married in your thirties is always better.

Text 2

I got married when I was 26 and my husband 28. It was a whirlwind romance and although my friends and family said they were delighted, they were also clearly shocked at the speed of events. There were even bets at the office where we both worked as to whether we'd last until Christmas. That was eight years ago and – at the risk of sounding super-smug – I am pleased to report that not only are we still together but we are still happy. Although marriage is usually part of a predictable progression within a relationship, for us to do something so ordinary seemed out-of-the-ordinary, partly because none of our friends had plans to settle down but mostly because neither had we until we met each other.

True or false: the writer was surprised at her own decision to marry in her twenties.

We saw marriage as the beginning of a great adventure. The first five years were spent having fun. We now have two beautiful daughters and a massive mortgage, and although I would be lying if I said we feel like love-struck teenagers every day, when times get tough we draw strength not only from each other but also from the knowledge that our family is built on foundations forged entirely from love, not convenience, body-clock-related desperation or unromantic inevitability.

Do the writer and her husband own their own house?

Our first year of marriage was probably the hardest as we learnt to adjust to the rhythm not only of each other but of married life. For example, he liked staying in bed. I rose with the lark. I liked long walks. He preferred short taxi rides. His ideal Sunday was in the pub watching football, mine in Ikea's soft furnishing department. I liked rock music. He liked Leonard Cohen.

True or false: the writer found it hard to get used to living with somebody who is different to her and also to being married.

We are still very distinct people but we have learnt to compromise and appreciate our differences. These days I am a connoisseur of the all-day lie-in, while he loves walking. I still hate football but realise that for him, hell is Ikea. We saw Leonard Cohen last month and both agreed it was the best concert ever. Neither of us can really remember what life was like before we met, and without wanting to sound too irritating, I think we'd have married even earlier had we met in time.

True or false: the writer thinks that a successful marriage is more about finding the right person than about marrying at a certain age.

4   Do the statements on the left answer the questions on the right? Put a tick when they do, and write 'not given' if they do not.

Statements	Questions	✓/not given
The report showed changing lifestyles and new opportunities for women.	According to the report, are women getting chances they did not have before?	1
The average age at first marriage for women is now two months before their thirtieth birthday.	Does this mean that women often have more than one marriage?	2
The proportion of babies born to those under twenty-five has halved since 1971.	Does this mean that fewer babies are being born?	3
Women now outnumber men in further and higher education.	Do we know if there are more women than men who continue their education after secondary school?	4

5 Read the statements and the text below and write TRUE if the text confirms the information, FALSE if the text says the opposite is true, or NOT GIVEN if there is not enough information in the text. Explain your answers.

Example: Unemployment is now worse than it has ever been over the last fourteen years. TRUE. The text says that unemployment is at a '14-year high'.

1 McDonald's is busy after school hours because young people are their main customers. _____

2 In McDonald's, customer satisfaction is partly dependent on who the customers are served by. _____

3 The majority of McDonald's employees are over 60. _____

4 The supermarkets Tesco, Asda and Sainsbury's are larger than Morrisons. _____

5 Morrisons supermarket is financially in a good position at the moment. _____

6 Two thirds of the jobs at Morrison will be taken up by people between the ages of 25 and 75. _____

7 Morrisons needs more people to work on their tills. _____

More than one in six young people are out of work, raising fears of a 'lost generation' of potential workers, as unemployment hit a 14-year high. Even McDonald's – a brand synonymous with today's youth – appeared to snub its main customer base with a new campaign to boost the recruitment of older staff. According to a Lancaster University study commissioned by the company, customer satisfaction was 20 per cent higher in those branches employing workers over 60. At present, 1,000 of McDonald's 75,000 workers in Britain are over 60.

Young people were granted some hope yesterday as Morrisons, Britain's fourth-largest supermarket, said that it would employ an extra 2,000 workers this year, having already surpassed the 5,000 jobs that it had said it would create this year. As job losses have mounted during the recession, supermarkets have been among the biggest recruiters. Morrisons said yesterday that a third of the new jobs would be filled by recruits aged 18 to 24. The jobs include vacancies for butchers, bakers and fishmongers as well as checkout operators. Morrisons trains staff through its own food academy and is aiming to have trained 100,000 workers to NVQ Level 2 by next spring.

Part 3: Exam practice

Do the following statements agree with the information given in the following text?

Write:
TRUE   if the text confirms the statement
FALSE   if the text confirms the opposite of the statement
NOT GIVEN   if it is impossible to know from the text

Statement	Your answer:
On average, women marry men who are older than them.	
Married couples in their forties are more likely to divorce than others.	
Women often stay at home while men go out to work.	
People in their thirties usually have not made much money yet.	
People's experiences in their previous relationships can damage their current relationships.	
People who marry in their thirties are pressured by their families to have children quickly.	

The trend is to get married later in life, but Andrew G. Marshall argues that the earlier you commit, the greater your chances of a long, happy partnership.

Over the past 35 years we have been waiting longer before settling down. According to the Office for National Statistics, men are getting married for the first time seven years later and women six years later. This means that the average man is aged 32 when he asks 'Will you marry me?' and the average woman is 29 when she says 'Yes'. But is this trend towards the thirty-something marriage making us happier and more satisfied? And when it comes to the forty-something crunch – the most common age for divorce – who is most vulnerable: those who took the plunge early at twenty-something or the ones who waited until thirty-something?

When couples seek my help as a marital therapist, I start by asking for the history of their relationship. People who married in their twenties often report tough times at the beginning: living with in-laws, financial problems or moving around the country as one partner climbed the career ladder. Also, couples who marry relatively early can grow apart, especially when one partner has been successful at work, travelled, met new people and grown in confidence while the other has been home-based.

However, the greatest threat to the twenty-something marriage is reaching 40 and wondering if the grass could be greener elsewhere. This is particularly dangerous when someone who married his or her first love starts fantasising about what he or she has missed. The temptation to have an affair can be overwhelming and very damaging. By contrast, the thirty-something marriage seems to sidestep these problems. At this age people are more established in careers and can start a relationship on a firm financial footing. They have a clearer idea of who they are and what they need from a relationship. When these couples reach their forties, they are less likely to be nostalgic or curious about the single life.

Yet, when faced with forty-something couples in crisis, I always feel more optimistic about the outcome for those who married in their twenties than those who married in their thirties. Why should this be? If you marry later, you are more likely to bring old baggage into your relationship. In some cases, I help couples to unravel the influence of someone from maybe two or three relationships back. For example, to someone who once had a suspicious partner – forever quizzing them about their movements – an innocent inquiry such as 'What time will you be back?' can sound aggressive.

Another problem of marrying later is higher expectations. This is because one of the best ways of recovering from a failed relationship and starting to look again is to tell yourself: 'I deserve better', or 'Next time I'll meet Mr or Miss Right'. There is nothing wrong with this strategy. But unfortunately, if the next relationship does not deliver, the bitterness becomes that bit greater and the desire for perfection that bit stronger.

The final issue about getting married at thirty-something, particularly your late thirties, is the need to start a family almost immediately. Many couples have no time to get to know each other properly or put down solid roots together. If a relationship has been built on long weekend lie-ins and brunches, the demands of small children can be a shock. This sense of isolation is worse if the grandparents are correspondingly older, too, and not fit enough to help.

Although the ultimate deciding factor for the success of a relationship is the character, determination and generosity of each partner (and that is not determined by age), my advice is always to seize the day and commit.

9 Community spirit

Exam focus: Matching information
Aims: Identifying sections of a text where information can be found
Identifying different types of information | Summarising a paragraph
Identifying the function of a paragraph

Part 1: Vocabulary

1 Look at the diagram and put the words a–g in order of size, 1–7, starting with the smallest place.

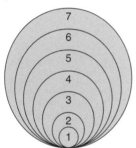

a city	**e** neighbourhood
b country	**f** street
c county	**g** suburb
d house	

1 _____   4 _____   7 _____
2 _____   5 _____
3 _____   6 _____

2 Match the pictures 1–4 with the words a–d.

a a cream tea _____   **c** an allotment _____
b a village green _____   **d** bunting _____

3 Match the words 1–6 with the definitions a–f.

1	a neighbourhood ____	a	an organisation of people interested in a particular activity or subject who usually meet on a regular basis
2	a community ____	b	a number of people or things which are together in one place at one time
3	a club ____	c	all the people who live in a particular area or place
4	an association ____	d	an official group of people, for example a political party, a business, a charity, or a club
5	a group ____	e	an official group of people who have the same occupation, aim or interest
6	an organisation ____	f	one of the parts of a town where people live

4 Complete the passage with the words a–h.

a associations   **d** cream tea   **g** neighbour
b bunting   **e** green   **h** plumbers
c communities   **f** groups

The Big Lunch is a new initiative that aims to bring neighbours and (1) _____ together by stringing up (2) _____ and sharing a plate of sandwiches and a (3) _____. More than 7,200 people have been busy setting up Big Lunches across the UK.

One of these events is being organised in the village of Wolvercote, three miles from Oxford, on the (4) _____, and they are expecting 300 people.

'We want to create a chance for people to meet their immediate (5) _____, and we also want to mix up the different (6) _____ in the area. It's all about getting people to shop locally, as well as join groups such as allotment (7) _____,' says the organiser. Planned events include face-painting and composting classes, and there will be stalls selling home-grown food and elder-flower champagne.

The Big Lunch can be beneficial in other ways, too. It's a great way to find reputable (8) _____, mechanics, painters or decorators.

5 Underline at least ten words or phrases related to the topic of neighbourhoods and communities in the passage. Use your dictionary if necessary.

The Prince of Wales is backing a campaign by 250,000 volunteers to save Britain from unsightly development and clutter.

The initiative, entitled Street Pride, aims to mobilise communities into taking an active role to prevent local roads, squares and precincts being spoiled. Backed by 1,000 civic groups across the nation, the organisers say that they want to create a vibrant body of activists.

Griff Rhys Jones, the comedy actor and presenter, will act as the figurehead for the campaign, which will be supported by English Heritage, the well-known organisation that protects and promotes England's historic built environment.

There are already many local campaigns. Activists in Tonbridge, Kent, are determined to restart the high street clock to re-assert its importance as a landmark in the town and in St Albans, locals are opposing a warehouse development.

Elsewhere there are plans to provide good playgrounds and save open spaces for community recreation. A priority will be to work with schools and to inspire children from an early age to value their local streets and distinctive buildings.

6   Find words in Exercise 5 that collocate with the words in the tables.

Adjectives	Nouns
active	1 _____
civic	2 _____
3 _____	campaign
4 _____	spaces
distinctive	5 _____

Verbs	Nouns
back	6 _____
mobilise	7 _____

7   Which word in Exercise 5 means ...

1   things that fill a place in an untidy way? _____

2   related to the duties or feelings that people have because they belong to a particular community? _____

3   an organised group of people who deal with something officially? _____

4   people who work to bring about political or social changes by campaigning in public or working for an organisation? _____

5   a person who is recognised as being the leader of an organisation or movement, although they have little real power? _____

8   Complete the tables with the correct word forms.

Noun	Adjective
suburb	1 _____
charity	2 _____

Noun	Noun (person)
action	6 _____
7 _____	a campaigner

Verb	Noun
participate	3 _____
initiate	4 _____
5 _____	a volunteer

9   Complete the sentences 1–4 with words from Exercise 8.

1   Hundreds of independent schools could lose their _____ status unless they increase fees.

2   The charity is supporting a(n) _____ to bring together global leaders, college and university students, and private citizens to identify global challenges and solutions.

3   Because of the recession, many local councils are selling residential property in _____ areas of large cities.

4   In her youth, she was a(n) _____ and _____ for black civil rights.

Part 2: Practice exercises

 Exam information: Matching information
In this type of task you need to match specific information, for example a reason, a description, an explanation, to the section of a text where it can be found.

The text is divided into sections which are labelled A, B, C, etc. Your answer to the questions is the letter of the relevant section.

The questions do not follow the order of the information in the text.

1   Read the text fragments 1–4. What are they about? Choose from the options, a, b, or c.

> **1**   Everybody knows the positive influence a good school in the neighbourhood can have on property prices. So, what do you do when you don't have one?

   a   the importance of good schools

   b   rising property prices

   c   the price of education

> **2**   A group of residents in Bolnore, near Haywards Heath, West Sussex, decided to build a school themselves. They successfully bid to start an eco-school in local woodlands. The parent-led group has just appointed a headteacher; the primary school, with space for 210 pupils, will open in September.

   a   applying for jobs in primary schools

   b   the power of parents

   c   environmentally-friendly building

> **3**   The group is just one of a growing number across the country: people banding together to improve their way of life, from saving a village shop or pub to starting a shared agriculture scheme, where everyone helps out and gets fresh vegetables weekly.

   a   the importance of healthy eating

   b   the disappearance of traditional village life

   c   the trend of taking action

> **4**   Across Britain, a community spirit is growing. The fact that most of the schemes are also green adds to their appeal. So, what is going on, and could you do the same in your area?

   a   the attraction of green schemes

   b   a call to action

   c   growing your own vegetables

Exam tip: In this type of exam task, you do not have to say what a whole paragraph is about. You have to find specific information in a paragraph.

2   Match the information underlined in the sentences 1–6 with the type of specific information.

1 London's East End community has changed. The old family structure – <u>in which mums had a lot of influence and sons followed dads down the docks</u> – is officially dead.	a reason
2 Many of those interviewed come across as model citizens. <u>Their children are better disciplined</u>, they're starting to achieve good grades and, in sharp contrast to the first generation, they see this place as home.	b explanation
3 The authors draw some important conclusions from all this. <u>Their main recommendation is a fresh approach to the culture of entitlement</u>.	c example
4 The study found that among white families running their own businesses, a strong sense of community endures. <u>Working together encourages mutual support</u>.	d comparison
5 Step back another half-century and you find a different scene: <u>a place inhabited by up to 150,000 Jewish immigrants</u>.	e summary
6 <u>Like some of the street markets that have sprung back to life in the past few years</u>, the community could, over time, reinvent itself.	f description

3   Underline examples of the types of information a–d in Text 1 and e–g in Text 2. You should be able to find them in the order they are listed and you may find more than one example.

a   a reason   **c**   details   **e**   a comparison   **g**   an explanation

b   an example   **d**   a summary   **f**   a description

Text 1

As I have worked with volunteers and volunteer groups for many years, I can vouch for the fact that the community spirit is flourishing. Every day I watch volunteers interacting with their fellow human beings, and in so doing, enriching themselves in so many ways.

I work in Manchester, and my job is placing volunteers with hospices, old age homes, and care homes for children. Our volunteers range in age from 17 to 70 and come from a wide range of backgrounds, but they are all willing to give up their time in order to help others. They are proof, if proof is needed, that we live in a rich multicultural environment. Volunteering is one of the most powerful forces for good in our society.

Text 2

Don't forget the power of local government when it comes to issues in your neighbourhood. In geometry, the shortest distance between two points is a straight line. In politics, if you have a local issue, take the shortest route and go first to your local council. Some issues are far better dealt with at community level. I live in an area where there is lack of infrastructure, lack of amenities, and a risk of flooding. There is a tendency to become quite angry if such issues are not dealt with. Keeping calm and electing the most level-headed member of the group as spokesperson will help your cause.

Another big problem is ghost estates, neighbourhoods with half-empty or empty buildings. Residents should ask their local politicians what will happen to these developments and how they plan to make things better.

4 The passage below has three paragraphs a–c. Which paragraphs mention the following? You may use any letter more than once.

1 a rescue operation _____
2 the high numbers of disappearing facilities _____
3 an example of a fund-raising activity _____

a
According to the Rural Shops Alliance, 600 country shops closed last year. Add the post office closure programme into the mix and thousands of neighbourhood hubs are being lost.

b
The people of Avebury, in Wiltshire, are among those trying to reverse the process. In April last year, their village shop closed when the adjoining post office shut down. Last Sunday, however, it reopened. The villagers, led by a small steering group, banded together to raise enough money to save it: 241 people bought £10 shares, with £3,000 coming from local donations and £25,000 from charitable schemes.

c
The National Trust, the organisation which owns the building, offered a minimal rent, a local blacksmith and carpenter made the shop sign and fitted out the interior, and one volunteer bakes cakes to sell. The shop, manned by a part-time manager and more than 30 volunteers, will stock everyday items such as sweets and washing-up liquid, as well as newspapers and fresh bread. There will also be post office facilities four half-days a week.

5 There are some reading strategies that help you match information. Are the sentences 1–6 good strategies or not? Write Y (yes) or N (no).

1 You should bear in mind that the numbered questions are paraphrases of bits of information in the paragraphs. _____
2 Before looking for detailed information, it is a good idea to have a general idea what is in the paragraphs first, so you should skim-read the text first to find out. _____
3 When working with paraphrases, underlining key words in the questions can help. _____
4 If you keep the questions or key words in mind when you are reading, you are more likely to find the information you are looking for. _____
5 If you have found an answer in a paragraph, you should look for the answer to the next question in the next paragraph. _____
6 You should answer the questions in the order they are given. _____

Check the answers to this exercise before doing the same type of task again in Exercise 6.

6 Use appropriate strategies to help you do the task.

The passage below has three paragraphs, labelled a–c. Which paragraphs mention the following? You may use any letter more than once.

1 a countryside issue _____
2 an example of a successful protest _____
3 a reason why pubs close _____
4 an organisation that encourages partnerships _____
5 a well-known person _____

a

According to recent figures from the British Beer & Pub Association, 39 pubs close every week. These days, it's far cheaper to buy alcohol in supermarkets to drink at home than it is to visit the local boozer. But that's not deterring the drinkers who are banding together to save their local pubs.

b

In Hesket Newmarket, Cumbria, 125 people raised £1,500 each and bought the Old Crown: each of them now has a say in how it is run. The pub in Charlton Horethorne, Dorset, was virtually derelict and about to be turned into a car park until the village rallied, set up a 'save the pub' group and had planning permission for the car park turned down: the Kings Arms reopened for business earlier this month. There are other examples up and down the country.

c

'The rural pub is the heart of the community – we've got to keep it as the heart,' says Pub Is the Hub, a scheme initiated by the Prince of Wales, which encourages breweries, pub owners, licensees and local communities to work together to support pubs in isolated rural areas. Pub Is the Hub (www.pubisthehub.org.uk) offers support and suggestions on how to go about things: it has assisted more than 350 pubs since its formation in 2001.

Part 3: Exam practice

*The following passage has seven paragraphs, labelled **A–G**. Which paragraphs mention the following information? You do not need to mention all the paragraphs.*

1 the relationship between local environment and behaviour _____

2 the benefits of asking around _____

3 becoming an organiser _____

4 partnerships against crime _____

5 problems which are not really problems _____

6 aspects of neighbourhood research _____

Will you love your neighbours?

A

When you are interested in buying a house, it's easy to check the location and specifications of the house, but how can you assess an area's community spirit – not just if the neighbours are friendly, but whether people will get involved in helping to deliver public services, setting up social enterprises and tackling local issues? Here are some tips for finding out what an area's community spirit is like.

B

If an estate agent shows you around, ask for the vendor's phone number. 'Meeting the seller is an opportunity to find out what an area is like,' says Chris Gittins, manager of Streets Alive (streetsalive.org.uk), which works with residents, councils and voluntary groups to build communities by hosting events and activities in streets. It is also worth trying to meet the neighbours to find out more about an area. If you don't find anyone at home, or don't get a clear response, talk to people in the pub or the corner shop.

C

Living Streets (livingstreets.org.uk), which promotes safe, active and enjoyable streets, says steer clear of heavy traffic. Its research shows that people living on busy streets shield themselves from noise, don't go outside and restrict their children's independence – all of which reduces interaction with neighbours. And although an open space may seem like an asset, it can also become a source of conflict, says Dominic Church, senior adviser at the Commission for Architecture and the Built Environment. 'If they are not kept clear and nobody is clearly responsible for the maintenance, they can become breeding grounds for graffiti, antisocial behaviour and kids mucking about,' he says.

D

Local police can tell you whether there is a Neighbourhood (or Home) Watch scheme in your area (mynhw.co.uk). Living in an area with a scheme doesn't just reduce your insurance premiums and ensure that the police tackle local issues such as theft: research shows that even when neighbours have nothing in common they share a desire to create a safe area and create a community spirit. If there isn't a scheme, find out why.

E

Councils have lists of local voluntary organisations that can help to reveal the interests and activities of local communities. Some councils also run award schemes, which may include prizes for active and inspirational groups. Search the web, use social media and post queries on forums to find out residents' views. This may give you more varied and up-to-date information than the council. Look at newschoolsnetwork.org to see if there are any plans to set up a new free school in the area. This is a sign of socially engaged parents and community motivation.

F

Floods, high crime levels and other issues can give a neighbourhood a bad image, but they can boost community spirit. In my case, the floods of 2007 brought people together to tackle climate change, which led to a low-carbon group that this year won two national competitions worth more than £800,000. The CrimeMapper website (maps.police.uk) provides information on crime and antisocial behaviour by area and police force. You can search by five types of crime and get details of your local neighbourhood policing team, its contacts, and the next 'Have Your Say' meeting.

G

If you are confident about the house, you could go ahead with the purchase and hold a street party to boost community spirit. 'People who have just moved into a house are critical to setting up street parties,' Gittins says. 'After two or three years it becomes harder – they meet neighbours, get set in their routines, and feel less motivated.'

10 On the move

Exam focus: Identifying writers' views or claims | Answering yes/no/not given questions

Aims: Working out the meaning of unfamiliar words | Working with paraphrases
Understanding the difference between fact and opinion

Part 1:   Vocabulary

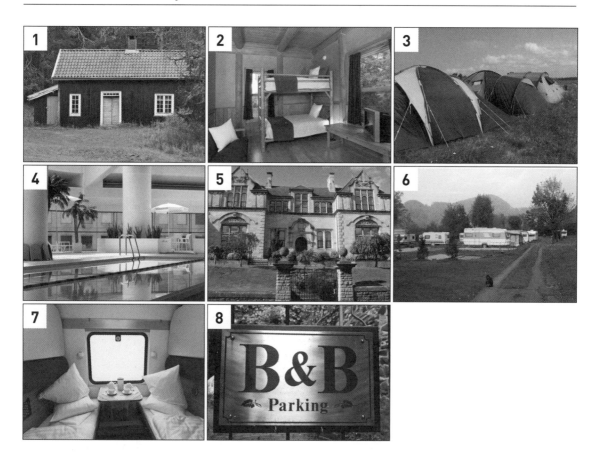

1   Match the pictures 1–8 to the words a–h.

a a bed and breakfast _____   **e** a resort _____
b a camp site _____   **f** a sleeper train _____
c a caravan park _____   **g** a stately home _____
d a cottage _____   **h** a youth hostel _____

2 Underline the words or phrases that are related to the topics of transport or tourism in the short texts 1–7.

> **1** Medium-size cars have become less popular in recent years, so many more crashes involve a big vehicle hitting a small one.

> **2** The study found that the rise in sales of 4x4s and people-carriers was causing more than 20 extra deaths and serious injuries a year among people in small cars.

> **3** There is massive public demand for bicycle lanes. A lot of people who are new to cycling think they are the only way they can be safe on the road, but what is really needed is for drivers to be trained to interact safely with cyclists, and cyclists to understand how to travel in congested traffic.

> **4** According to the council, a number of areas have been identified where maintenance has been poor and there are obstacles in the cycle paths. It claims to be addressing the problems.

> **5** He believes measures such as the ban on trucks in the city centre and the bicycle rental and bike-to-work schemes have been more effective in promoting cycling.

> **6** Travel is about gaining a greater understanding of other cultures: in today's survey 70% said it was important to experience cultures in other countries.

> **7** North America and Britain are Ireland's strongest tourist markets.

3 Make collocations with the words in 1–5 and words or phrases from the texts in Exercise 2. The definition of the word or phrase you are looking for is in brackets.

Example: a rise in sales (an increase in)

1 _____ demand (very large in size, quantity, or extent)

2 _____ traffic (extremely crowded and blocked with vehicles and people)

3 _____ maintenance (of a low quality or standard, in bad condition)

4 _____ a problem (to try to understand or deal with)

5 _____ an understanding (to gradually get more of something)

4 Work out the meaning of the words in italics in the sentences 1–3 by studying their context.

1 Most 4x4s and many luxury *saloons* and people carriers would be included and would pay £320 a year, compared with the present top rate of £170.

   a a place where alcoholic drinks are sold and drunk
   b a car with seats for four or more people, a fixed roof, and a boot that is separated from the rear seats
   c a large handbag with shoulder straps, usually used as a travel bag

2 The deaths and injuries caused by drink-drivers every year not only devastate families, but also impose a huge economic *burden*: the average cost to society of each road death is over a million pounds.

    a an advantage, especially in terms of financial, economic or business interests

    b the price of goods

    c a problem or a responsibility that causes someone a lot of difficulty, worry, or hard work

3 If there were a law prohibiting new drivers from having passengers or travelling after dark, accidents might be avoided, but it would be difficult to *enforce*.

    a to make something stronger or more intense, sometimes resulting in increased difficulties

    b to make sure that a law is obeyed, usually by punishing people who do not obey it

    c to continue doing something enjoyable

5   **Underline synonyms of the words or phrases in italics in the short texts 1–6.**

> **1** In tourism, you have to make a decision about the kind of *clientele* you want: either you attract customers with money or you don't.

> **2** The Department of Finance would argue that the tax on departing passengers encourages more Irish people to holiday at home. But any gains to the tourism sector from *'staycations'* are likely to be outweighed by the loss of business from tourists.

> **3** The tourism business, on the other hand, is worth an estimated £6.3 billion to Ireland each year, and has been identified as a *sector* that could help the country out of recession.

> **4** The transport minister wants to increase the number of people who travel to work by bicycle. Just 2% of *commuters* use bikes, and he wants this to increase to 10%.

> **5** The country's cycling lanes are 'worse than useless' and need to be removed, *a lobby group* has claimed, but a council spokesperson said: 'I think we have to look at countries such as Denmark, where they are building lanes differently. This isn't always what cycle campaigners want, but that's the way we're going to have to go.'

> **6** We believe that introducing this *arrangement* in Britain would significantly reduce road *casualties*, and academics agree. Cardiff University published research this week that said the scheme would prevent 200 deaths and 1,700 serious injuries every year and save the economy £890 million.

6   **When you learn the meaning of a word which is common in academic texts, it is a good idea to also look up the different word forms. What nouns are formed by the verbs 1–7? Use a dictionary if necessary.**

Verb	Noun
collide	**1** _____
enforce	**2** _____
interact	**3** _____
involve	**4** _____
congest	**5** _____
encounter	**6** _____
constitute	**7** _____

Part 2: Practice exercises

 Exam information: Yes/No/Not Given

This task tests whether you understand the writer's point of view.

The questions are in the form of statements, all of which express an opinion. You have to read the text to find out if the writer expresses the opinion in the statement or not.

- If the writer expresses it, your answer will be YES.
- If the writer contradicts the statement, your answer will be NO.
- If it is impossible to know from the text if the writer expresses the opinion or not, your answer will be NOT GIVEN.

The information in the text will be in the same order as the questions.

1 An opinion does not have to be based on fact or knowledge and we cannot prove it right or wrong. Read the statements 1–3 and write F if the statement is a fact or O if it expresses an opinion.

   1 Frankfurt International airport serves the most international destinations. _____
   2 Thai Airways has the best airport services. _____
   3 Thai Airways has won a prize for the 'Best Airport Services'. _____

2 Read the short text and the statements 1–3. Write YES if the statement is expressed in the text or NO if it is not. For each statement, underline the one word in the text that helped you determine whether the answer was YES or NO.

> Since then, controls on outbound travel have been relaxed further, partly through the simplification of private passport and visa applications, which has helped the demand for independent travel, particularly among young people.

Example: Controls on outbound travel were already relaxed in the past. <u>YES</u> *('further')*

   1 Young people are the only group that want to travel independently. _____
   2 There is more than one way in which controls on outbound travel have been relaxed. _____
   3 The relaxation of the controls on outbound travel is only one of the reasons why the demand for independent travel has increased. _____

3 Read the passage. Then read the statements 1–5 and write YES if the statement expresses the writer's opinion or NO if it contradicts the writer's opinion.

   1 The reasons why the Chinese visited last year were, in order of importance, tourism, business and social reasons. _____
   2 Three reasons for visiting are Britain's historic buildings, shopping and Premier League football. _____
   3 The Chinese like luxury goods. _____
   4 Burberry, Gucci, Louis Vuitton and malt whisky are not basic items. _____
   5 People can buy luxury items in China at lower prices than in Britain. _____

Last year's visitors from China were split fairly evenly between holidaymakers, businessmen and people visiting friends and relatives. Britain's historic buildings and shopping are among the biggest attractions for holidaymakers, although the VisitBritain report highlights strong interest in Premier League football.

London's shopping emporia satisfy the Chinese appetite for luxury goods such as Burberry, Gucci and Louis Vuitton fashion items and malt whisky. Import tariffs and taxes mean that such goods are 30 per cent cheaper than the equivalent items in China — and they are less likely to be fakes.

Other big factors in the rising tide of Chinese visitors are the increasing ease and cheapness of travel, as new airports increase flight capacity, and the wider introduction by employers of paid leave and the easing of rules on taking money out of the country. In 2005, the UK was granted approved destination status, which opened up the market to groups on trips booked through licensed travel agents.

4   This type of exam task will often require you to identify paraphrases of the statements in the text. Read the text below and find words and expressions that have a similar meaning to the words and phrases 1–8. Be careful: they are not in the same order as in the passage.

1   a list that shows how successful an organisation is when it is compared to other similar organisations _____

2   an amount expressed as a number _____

3   to calculate the position that someone or something has on a scale _____

4   a decrease _____

5   an increase _____

6   to reach _____

7   to say that an event will happen _____

8   a statement of what is expected to happen in the future _____

After last year's fall in visitors, China ranked fortieth in Britain's inbound league table, while spending was down 14 per cent to £117 million, putting it 31st. However, spending per visit was up 3 per cent to £1,130 and VisitBritain predicts a rapid rise by 2014.

Official figures suggest that 26.8 million Chinese made overseas trips last year, the top destinations being Hong Kong, Macau, Singapore and South Korea. That figure is forecast to hit 100 million by 2020.

Exam tip: To help you decide if information is not given, read the statement first and then scan the text to find the topic you are looking for. You should not always expect to find the words or phrases used in the statement; instead look for synonyms. If you can find no information at all, then the answer is probably 'not given'. If there is information, then you need to work out if it actually expresses the writer's opinion.

5 Read the text in Exercise 3 again. Then read the statements 1–6 and write YES if the statement expresses the writer's opinion or NG (not given) if it is impossible to know what the writer's opinion is.

1 Chinese women do not travel for business. _____
2 Chinese travellers visit Buckingham Palace and the Tower of London. _____
3 Whiskies are cheaper in Britain than in China. _____
4 It is cheaper and easier for the Chinese to travel than in the past. _____
5 There are more airports than in the past. _____
6 More Chinese people can now travel because they are paid while on holiday. _____

6 Read the sentences 1–5. Then read the statements a–c and write YES if the statement is expressed in the text, NO if it contradicts the statement and NG (not given) if the information is not in the sentence.

1 One traveller in five is avoiding travel agents and buying holidays from home.
  a Twenty per cent of people are staying at home rather than booking a holiday through a travel agent. _____
  b Twenty per cent of travellers have had bad experiences with travel agents. _____
  c Twenty per cent of travellers are booking their holidays directly, without help from travel professionals. _____

2 Holiday companies say that customers are becoming more confident about booking packages by phone or over the Internet.
  a Travel agents have noticed that their customers are more confident than they used to be. _____
  b Travel agencies have noticed that people now feel more able to book their holidays online or by phone. _____
  c More holidays are booked by phone or over the Internet than by travel agents. _____

3 This puts increasing pressure on Britain's estimated 9,000 agents, which have already been suffering from competition from low-cost airlines.
  a The British travel industry has had some setbacks. _____
  b Travel agents do not understand that competition can be positive. _____
  c After competition from low-cost airlines, business is now getting better for travel agents. _____

4 The sales and marketing director of the Cosmos company said that travel agents will have to be faster on their feet and closer to their customers to survive.
  a The sales and marketing director thinks that travel agents have always been slow to react. _____
  b The sales and marketing director thinks that travel agents are at risk of having to close. _____
  c The sales and marketing director thinks that travel agents react quickly to customers' needs. _____

5 He added that in five years there will probably be a third fewer travel agents than now.
  a He said that there may be some more travel agencies in the future. _____
  b Five years from now, there are likely to be two thirds of the amount of travel agents there are now. _____
  c In the next decade a lot of travel agencies will go bankrupt. _____

Part 3: Exam practice

Read the following passage. Do the statements agree with the views of the writer? Write:

- **YES**   if the statement agrees with the views of the writer.
- **NO**   if the statement contradicts what the writer thinks.
- **NOT GIVEN**   if it is impossible to know what the writer's point of view is.

1 The route between Papa Westray and Westray is officially the shortest scheduled domestic flight in the world.

2 There is more than a mile between Papa Westray and Westray.

3 Loganair does not charge to fly Westray Junior High pupils to school.

4 Pupils from Papa Westray and from Westray go to Orkney to study for their Highers.

5 The airline claims that the flight is useful for tourists as well as residents.

6 Music, art, craft, physical education and home economics are rarely taught on the islands.

Some children moan about having to get a bus to school. Six teenagers on a remote Scottish island, however, have the rather more exciting prospect of going to school by plane on what is believed to be the world's shortest domestic flight.

The journey from Papa Westray to Westray in the Orkney Islands takes 96 seconds, covering a distance of just over a mile. With a tail wind, it can take as little as 47 seconds. Normally the teenagers go by ferry but when the vessel was taken out of service for refurbishment, Loganair, an airline company, stepped in and offered to fly them to Westray Junior High.

Six students, all aged 13-14, will be flown to and from school until the end of the year when the ferry, the Golden Mariana, is scheduled to return, Loganair said.

Papa Westray has a population of 70 and no secondary school. Westray, home to more than 600 residents, has about 70 pupils enrolled at the junior high and nine full-time teachers. The school provides education to Standard Grade level. The six teenagers from Papa Westray take the flight every Tuesday morning, stay with host families for two nights and then catch a return flight on Thursday after school. Pupils from either island choosing to study for their Highers* must travel to Kirkwall, the capital of Orkney.

Loganair, which operates the eight-seater service in an Islander plane, has changed its schedule to ensure that the children get to school on time. The company said that the flight was the shortest in the world and with favourable tail winds could be over in less than a minute. The distance is shorter than the length of the main runway at Edinburgh Airport.

Jonathan Hinkles, the commercial director of the airline, said: 'While it is a popular tourist route for many visitors to Scotland, it is also a vital lifeline for those residents who live, work or do business in the Orkneys and it will make all the difference to ensuring that those children who live on Papa Westray can continue their schooling throughout the winter months.'

Willie McEwen, acting head teacher at Westray Junior High, said: 'We're delighted that Loganair has come forward with this solution. Our children will enjoy the flying especially as, at this time of the year, it can be quite rough on the boat. This kind of flexibility is an essential part of island life and the youngsters take it all in their stride.'

The Islander air service, which carries around 20,000 passengers each year, is critical for local residents during the winter months. It delivers food, mail and newspapers, and provides a lifeline between the islands and Kirkwall on mainland Orkney.

In addition, Loganair regularly carries visiting teachers out to the islands to lead lessons in subjects including music, art, craft, physical education and home economics.

The Guinness World Records said that it did not recognise the world's shortest scheduled domestic flight. "The category is currently under research," a spokesman said.

Glossary:
Highers: national school-leaving exams in Scotland

11 Cultural differences

Exam focus: Matching features
Aims: Identifying facts | Identifying opinions | Working with paraphrases
Skimming and scanning | Recognising connections between facts

Part 1: Vocabulary

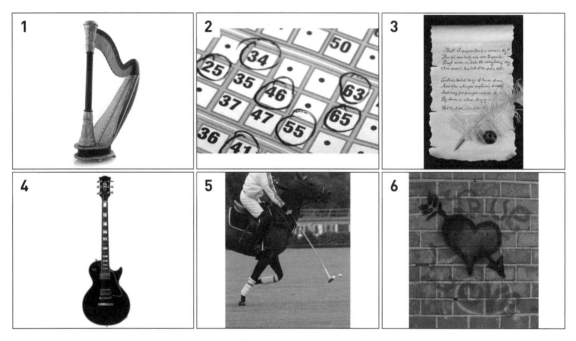

1 Match the pictures 1–6 above with the words a–f.

a a game of bingo _____   **c** a harp _____   **e** graffiti _____

b a game of polo _____   **d** an electric guitar _____   **f** poetry _____

2 A culture is a particular society or civilisation, especially considered in relation to its beliefs, way of life, or art. The word 'culture' also refers to activities such as the arts and philosophy, which are considered to be important for the development of civilisation and of people's minds. 'Low culture' refers to anything which appeals to most people, whereas 'high culture' refers to things which are highly valued in a society, especially by educated people.

Draw a table like the one on page 95 and put the words below into the group with which they are usually associated.

baked beans ballet basketball bestsellers bingo caviar champagne classical music
coin-collecting electric guitars gossip magazines graffiti horse-riding literary festivals
novels opera plays by Shakespeare poetry polo reality television rock concerts
romantic fiction slapstick humour soap operas take-away meals violins

Low culture	High culture

3 Underline at least fifteen words or phrases related to the topic of cultural activities in the text below. Use your dictionary if necessary.

How affordable is high culture? One great myth of our time is that tickets for opera, theatre, ballet and orchestral concerts are too expensive, especially for the young. This is infuriating as, in Britain, at least, it's nonsense. The cheap tickets to hear London's orchestras range from £7 to £9 – same as a cinema ticket, and lower than at many pop and comedy venues. For comparison, when the Los Angeles Philharmonic perform with top soloists and conductors the cheapest seat is £30; and at the Berlin Philharmonic it's an expensive £46.

Finding cheap tickets to the opera and ballet isn't so easy. True, British companies don't charge the stratospheric prices found on the Continent (£2,000 for a good seat at the premiere of La Scala's *Carmen* last December), but the tickets are still pretty steep. Plump fees paid to star performers partly account for that. Luckily, however, one spectacular technological innovation has stunningly transformed the scene. It's live (or slightly delayed) cinema transmissions. The New York Metropolitan Opera now beams its shows to 800 cinemas round the world, and British companies aren't far behind. Cinematic opera is excellent value. For the cost of a good bottle of wine (£10 or £15 for the Royal Opera House's shows; £25 for the Met) you can sit in your local movie-house and see a high-definition relay of what's occurring on the world's grandest stages. No, it's not the same as being there. But in some ways it's better. The sound is impeccable. The close-ups, particularly of dancers, are enthralling. And you can react to the show as part of a live audience, rather than sitting on your own at home.

To me, this mountain of evidence, together with free museum admissions, indicates that the arts world should stop worrying that its audiences are still mostly middle-class. Anyone who can afford to visit a pub can also afford to see top-quality drama, music and dance. The real battle now should be ensuring that schoolchildren are given enough tastes of high culture to make them want to buy all those cheap tickets when they grow up.

4 Match words from the text in Exercise 3 above with their definitions a–k.

a a belief or explanation that many people believe but which is actually untrue _____

b places where an event or activity will happen _____

c a person who stands in front of an orchestra or choir and directs its performance _____

d very high indeed _____

e expensive _____

f big, fat _____

g in an extremely impressive or attractive way _____

h to send (radio signals or television pictures) somewhere by means of electronic equipment _____

i a signal or broadcast _____

j perfect, with no faults _____

k fascinating _____

Exam tip: It is easy to forget the meaning of new words. Try to work with new words you come across: look at the different related meanings, look up the different word forms and use them in a sentence about yourself. The more you do with a word when you first come across it, the more likely you are to remember its meaning later.

5   Check your answers to Exercise 4 before you do this exercise. Think of your own examples for 1–6.

1   a myth that you believed for a long time

2   a venue that you have been to

3   someone you know who was a plump baby

4   someone who is stunningly beautiful

5   someone who has impeccable taste in clothes

6   a performance that you found enthralling

6   The words in italics in the sentences 1–4 are different forms of words from Exercise 3, with different but related meanings. Work out their meaning by studying their context in the sentences.

1   The rocket has passed the *stratosphere* and has entered outer space.

2   Let me *plump* your pillows so that you are more comfortable.

3   After her first performance, she *beamed* with pleasure.

4   We were *stunned* when we heard the tragic news.

7   Which answers from the text in Exercise 4 above can also have the meanings 1–4?

1   a substance that heat or electricity can pass through or along

2   a race between two or more teams, for example teams of runners or swimmers. Each member of the team runs or swims one section of the race.

3   rising at a very sharp angle and difficult to go up

4   a well-known story which was made up in the past to explain natural events or to justify religious beliefs or social customs

8   Write a paragraph about cultural events in your home town or country. You could write about the current situation or what you would like to change. Try to use all the words below. (They are from the text in Exercise 3.)

affordable   cinema   museum   spectacular   stunning   theatre   tickets   venue

Part 2: Practice exercises

 Exam information: Feature-matching

In this type of task, you will be asked to match a numbered list of factual statements or opinions to a group of features taken from a text.

This task tests your ability to identify opinions and recognise the connections between facts in a text.

The information contained in the list of statements is NOT in the order you read about it in the text.

1 Underline one fact and one opinion in the text.

> Art is more important than almost anything else. But it is also very difficult to do and often difficult to understand. So why should we pay for this high culture for the fun of a few? And, come to that, how should we pay? Answering those questions convincingly is now more urgent than ever. The government has recently announced that it will cut the arts budget, so we need to think about what can be done.

2 Identify some areas that are mentioned in the texts a–d. Text a has been done for you.

a

> A study commissioned by the Australian government to tackle obesity recommended this month that children under two should be banned from watching TV and electronic media such as computer games. It also said those aged two to five should watch no more than one hour a day, as exposure to TV at an early age could delay language development, affect concentration, and lead to obesity.

Areas mentioned: *research, Australia, obesity, young children, TV, computer games, children's development*

b

> For ten years the official advice to parents from the American Academy of Paediatrics has been that children under two should not see any electronic media. In 2000, a law was passed that requires all television units to have V-chip technology. This allows parents to block certain programmes based on their ratings category. A password prevents children from changing the settings.

Areas mentioned: _____

c

> Advertising junk food during young children's programmes was banned in Britain in 2007; this was later extended to all those aimed at under-16s. But health campaigners say children are still seeing the ads during adult shows and have called for a total pre-9 p.m. ban on junk food ads.

Areas mentioned: _____

d

> Over the past thirty years the globalisation of the economy has proceeded at a faster pace than ever. Customers, suppliers and employees often come from all over the globe, resulting in an increasingly diverse workforce and business environment. Managers routinely interact with and rate the performance of employees from diverse backgrounds. One country with an increasingly important role is China, which accounts for almost four per cent of world output and is a viable site for cross-cultural research on job performance.

Areas mentioned: _____

3 Skim-reading and scanning are useful techniques in tasks that require you to match features. For each paragraph, do the following:
   - Skim-read the paragraph and make a note about the topic(s) of each paragraph.
   - Make notes about the information in each paragraph.
   - Scan the text to make sure you have identified all the information about the West and about China. If necessary, add to your notes.

You should end up with an outline of the text.

> In Western literature, traditionally job performance appraisal systems were related to the completion of tasks specific to one's job. Chinese tradition, on the other hand, is rooted in collectivist philosophies such as the Confucian principles of benevolence, right conduct, loyalty and good manners. More than 2,000 years ago, Confucius described an ideal commonwealth state in which 'a sense of sharing displaces the effects of selfishness and materialism'. President Hu Jintao recently declared the importance of developing an 'advanced socialist culture'.
>
> Given these cultural differences, our study addressed two questions: whether the Chinese concept of counterproductive work behaviour is the same as in the West; and what relative importance Chinese and Western managers give to task performance and other work behaviours when assessing job performance.
>
> There were noticeable similarities between Chinese and Western managers in terms of what they considered to be counterproductive behaviour such as stealing from the organisation, which is frowned on in any work environment, Chinese or Western.
>
> But Chinese managers scored higher than Western managers on the importance placed on task completion and on individualistic aspects such as 'challenging work' and 'opportunity for advancement'. They rated equally with Western managers on aspects such as 'work with people who cooperate'. China has evolved from a centralised and planned economy to a decentralised and market-driven one in 20 years. It is possible that the increasingly competitive environment has forced organisations and managers to pay more attention to the completion of tasks to survive and succeed. It is also possible that Chinese people have generally become more individualistic during industrialisation.

4 In feature-matching tasks, synonyms and paraphrases are used to re-state information in the text. Paraphrase the phrases 1–4, which reflect ideas from the text in Exercise 3.

   1 our study addressed two questions
   2 stealing from the organisation is frowned on in any work environment
   3 they rated equally with Western managers
   4 organisations and managers need to pay more attention to the completion of tasks

5 Match the statements 1–5 with a–c. Refer your notes from Exercise 3, your paraphrases from Exercise 4, and the text if you need to.

1 There are historical documents available about attitudes regarding work culture. _____

2 Thefts from one's employer are regarded as unacceptable. _____

3 Managers did not give career progression the highest rating. _____

4 Team work is considered important. _____

5 There have been fundamental changes in the economy. _____

a	China
b	the West
c	both China and the West

6 Use the strategies you learnt in Exercises 1–5 and match the statements 1–4 with the facts and opinions a–d based on the text below.

1 The new theatre did not need more time or money to be built than had been predicted. _____

2 The new building does not live up to expectations. _____

3 The money to build the new theatre came from three different sources. _____

4 Performances are not about perfection but about sharing experiences. _____

a an opinion expressed by the writer
b an opinion expressed by the company or its representative
c a statement of fact by the writer
d a statement of fact by the company or its representative

The newly rebuilt Royal Shakespeare Theatre in Stratford-upon-Avon is on budget and on time, a message which has been repeated often by all the directors, theatre consultants, project managers and PRs showing people round the new building. But it is also deeply disappointing.

You see, there's more to theatre than the play. Drama starts at the front door, and should unfold every step towards your seat. The lobby, the stairs, the loos: they're all part of it. Shakespeare understood this: Elizabethan theatres were marvellous, fantastical, riotous places. Great theatre designers understood it and some modern companies understand it, and drama is present in whole buildings – loos, lobbies and all. There should be intrigue, seduction and surprise. Great theatre, great theatres, should transport you to another world the second you enter. And by another world, I don't mean something that feels like the local council sports centre.

Today, though, theatres can't just be theatres. They have, the consultants say, to be 'revenue generators', open, friendly, accessible and transparent.

But the Royal Shakespeare Company had a problem: money. They first wanted to demolish the entire building for an 'iconic' replacement by the fashionable Dutch architect Erick van Egeraat. In the end they decided to build a new theatre within the skin of the old: £112.8 million was raised, a third privately, two thirds from the Arts Council and the regional development agency. This seems like a lot of money. However, to rebuild completely a major national – no, world – theatre within the shell of an old one on a very tricky site, it's not much money at all. And it shows.

Theatre, says the RSC's artistic director, Michael Boyd, is about experiences 'shared in the same space in real time'. That's exactly what architecture should be, and what the Royal Shakespeare Theatre is not. 'The theatre experiences we most enjoy,' he adds, 'are the ones with loads of problems but bags of character.' I wonder if he is being ironic.

Part 3:   Exam practice

Match the statements 1–6, which describe number systems in different cultures, with the cultures and languages A–F.

1 In this community, people do not really learn how to count, because there is no need for them to learn.   _____

2 The most used system was started by these people.   _____

3 The counting system in this culture works with small sets but uses addition.   _____

4 The situation in this community demonstrates that people can estimate quantities even in cultures where exact numbers do not exist.   _____

5 The system here has been in existence for a very long time but may not be the best one.   _____

6 The counting system in this culture is different from that in most other cultures.   _____

A	Pirahã
B	Munduruku
C	Yupno
D	Waimirí
E	English
F	Indian

In *Rarities in Numeral Systems*, Harald Hammarström lists 12 South American languages that lack exact numbers above one. He prefers to call these systems 'one-few-many', since there are usually words in these languages for 'few' and 'many'. He also mentions two languages that have no exact numbers. The most studied of these is Pirahã, which is spoken by only about 400 people. It has a word for 'about one' and a word for 'about two'. As if that wasn't fuzzy enough, the words for 'about one' and 'about two' are the same – hoi – the only difference being a change in inflection.

The Amazonian Indians whose sense of number has been most closely studied are the Munduruku, who have numerical words only up to five. Animals and babies are good at discriminating quantities above five, so one would expect that the Indians are too – even though they do not have words to express such amounts. And this is exactly what experiments conducted by the French linguist Pierre Pica have confirmed: when given tests that involve comparing sets of more than five dots on a screen, the Munduruku scored just as high as Westerners. When Pica looked more closely at the Munduruku's number words, he realised that only their words for one and two were used with any sense of exactness. The words for three, four and five were approximations – as if what they meant to say was 'threeish', 'fourish' and 'fiveish'. In this aspect, the Munduruku are just like the 'one-two-many' tribes, who also have exact numbers only up to two.

When Indians do learn numbers, in fact, they appear uninterested by them. A Pirahã girl was once taken out of the village to receive medical treatment. During her time with Brazilians she learnt some Portuguese and how to count in Portuguese. No problem. But after returning to the community, while she retained some Portuguese she quickly forgot how to count.

Anthropologists first reached communities on the other side of the world, in Papua New Guinea, in the late nineteenth century. They discovered that they used not just their fingers to count but also their whole bodies. The natives started out with the fingers and thumb of one hand for one to five, but then carried on for higher numbers with wrist, elbow, shoulders, sternum and so on. For example, one tribe, the Yupno, go as high as 34: their word for 34 is 'one dead man'. These Papuan 'body-tally' systems are unusual because almost all other systems group numbers in much smaller sets.

In the Amazon there are also tribes with bases of two, three and four. For example, the Waimirí have words for one to three, and then say '3+1', '3+2', '3+3', '3+3+1', '3+3+2' and '3+3+3'.

Our base ten system of the digits zero to nine, which has its origins in India, is now in use all over the developed world. It is a natural system, but for several hundred years mathematicians have questioned whether it is the wisest base for us to have. The campaign for adding two new numbers, so that our system becomes base 12, is still active – the argument is to do with the extra divisibility of 12 compared with ten, since 12 can be divided by two, three, four and six while ten can be divided only by two and five. In fact, there are humans that already use base 12: and almost all of them belong to the tribes of the Plateau area of northern Nigeria.

12 Practice test

On pages 103–113 you will find an example of what the IELTS Reading exam looks like.

Taking this practice test under timed conditions will give you an idea of what it will be like to take the actual exam.

You have one hour to complete the exam. This includes the time required to write your answers on an answer sheet. There are three passages, so aim to spend about twenty minutes on each of them.

Exam tips:
- Do not worry about unfamiliar vocabulary or topics, but do not relax if you are familiar with the subject of a passage: the answers should be in the passage itself.
- Check if the passages have glossaries.
- Read the instructions carefully. They may look similar to instructions from practice tasks, but there may be important differences. Check to see if an example is given.
- Skip any questions you are not sure about, rather than wasting too much time on a particular question. You can come back to those questions later.
- Try to give an answer for all the questions. Multiple choice questions in particular are worth trying to answer, as you have a chance of guessing the correct one.

READING PASSAGE 1

*You should spend about 20 minutes on **Questions 1–13** which are based on Reading Passage 1 below:*

Affordable Art

Art prices have fallen drastically. The art market is being flooded with good material, much of it from big-name artists, including Pablo Picasso and Andy Warhol. Many pieces sell for less than you might expect, with items that would have made £20,000 two years ago fetching only £5,000 to £10,000 this autumn, according to Philip Hoffman, chief executive of the Fine Art Fund. Here, we round up what is looking cheap now, with a focus on works in the range of £500 to £10,000.

Picasso is one of the most iconic names in art, yet some of his ceramics and lithographs fetched less than £1,000 each at Bonhams on Thursday. The low prices are because he produced so many of them. However, their value has increased steadily and his works will only become scarcer as examples are lost.

Nic McElhatton, the chairman of Christie's South Kensington, says that the biggest 'affordable' category for top artists is 'multiples' – prints such as screenprints or lithographs in limited editions. In a Christie's sale this month, examples by Picasso, Matisse, Miró and Steinlen sold for less than £5,000 each.

Alexandra Gill, the head of prints at the auction house, says that some prints are heavily hand-worked, or often coloured, by the artist, making them personalised. 'Howard Hodgkin's are a good example,' she says. 'There's still prejudice against prints, but for the artist it was another, equal, medium.'

Mr Hoffman believes that these types of works are currently about as 'cheap as they can get' and will hold their value in the long run – though he admits that their sheer number means prices are unlikely to rise any time soon.

It can be smarter to buy really good one-offs from lesser-known artists, he adds. A limited budget will not run to the blockbuster names you can obtain with multiples, but it will buy you work by Royal Academicians (RAs) and others whose pieces are held in national collections and who are given long write-ups in the art history books. For example, the Christie's sale of art from the Lehman Brothers collection on Wednesday will include *Valley with cornflowers* in oil by Anthony Gross (22 of whose works are held by the Tate), at £1,000 to £1,500. There is no reserve on items with estimates of £1,000 or less, and William Porter, who is in charge of the sale, expects some lots to go for 'very little'. The sale also has oils by the popular Mary Fedden (whose works are often reproduced on greetings cards), including *Spanish House* and *The White Hyacinth*, at £7,000 to £10,000 each.

Large works by important Victorian painters are available in this sort of price range, too. These are affordable because their style has come to be considered 'uncool', but they please a large traditionalist following nonetheless. For example, the sale of 19th-century paintings at Bonhams on Wednesday has a Hampstead landscape by Frederick William Watts at £6,000 to £8,000 and a study of three Spanish girls by John Bagnold Burgess at £4,000 to £6,000. There are proto-social realist works depicting poverty, too, such as *Uncared For* by Augustus Edwin Mulready, at £10,000 to £15,000.

Smaller auction houses offer a mix of periods and media. Tuesday's sale at Chiswick Auctions in West London includes a 1968 screenprint of *Campbell's Tomato Soup* by Andy Warhol, at £6,000 to £8,000, and 44 sketches by Augustus John, at £200 to £800 each. The latter have been restored after the artist tore them up. Meanwhile, the paintings and furniture sale at Duke's of Dorchester on Thursday has a coloured block print of *Acrobats at Play* by Marc Chagall, at £100 to £200, and a lithograph of a mother and child by Henry Moore, at £500 to £700. A group of five watercolour landscape studies by Jean-Baptiste Camille Corot is up at £1,500 to £3,000.

Affordable works from lesser-known artists and younger markets are less safe, but they have the potential to offer greater rewards if you catch an emerging trend. Speculating on such trends is high-risk, so is worthwhile only if you like what you buy (you get something beautiful to keep, whatever happens), can afford to lose the capital and enjoy the necessary research.

A trend could be based on a country or region. China has rocketed, but other Asian and Middle Eastern markets have yet to really emerge. Mr Horwich mentions some 1970s Iraqi paintings that he sold this year in Dubai. 'They are part of a sophisticated scene that remains little-known.' Mr Hoffman tips Turkey and the Middle East. Meanwhile, the Sotheby's Impressionist and modern art sale in New York features a 1962 oil by the Vietnamese Vu Cao Dam, a graduate of Hanoi's École des Beaux Arts de l'Indochine and friend of Chagall, at $8,000 to $12,000 (£5,088 to £7,632). The painting shows two girls boating in traditional *ao dai* dresses.

A further way of making money is to try to spot talent in younger artists. The annual Frieze Art Fair in Regent's Park provides a chance to buy from 170 contemporary galleries. Or you could gamble on the future fame trajectory of an established artist's subject. For example, a Gerald Laing screenprint of *The Kiss* (2007) showing Amy Winehouse and her ex-husband is up for £4,700 at the Multiplied fair.

QUESTIONS 1–5

Use information from the passage to complete the table below. Use **NO MORE THAN TWO WORDS** from the passage for each space.

Example of artist	Name of work/Type of art form	Reason for low price
1 _____	ceramics and lithographs	he produced many
2 _____	Valley with cornflowers	3 _____
John Bagnold Burgess	a study of three Spanish girls	4 _____
Vu Cao Dam	5 _____	Asian region (except China) is not popular at the moment

QUESTIONS 6–9

*Choose one of the endings (i–viii) from the **List of Endings** to complete each sentence below. Write the appropriate letters next to questions 6–9. The information in the completed sentences should accurately reflect what is said in the text.*

***NB** There are more endings (i–viii) than sentence beginnings, so you will not need to use them all. You may use each ending once only.*

6   'Multiples' are … _____

7   Prints are … _____

8   Gross and Fedden are … _____

9   Victorian painters are … _____

List of Endings

i   artists that have never been popular at all.

ii   hand-made and personal art works.

iii   items that are not really popular with buyers but good value for money.

iv   artists that seem to like real life topics.

v   top artists that sell many works.

vi   artists who have used a particular type of material.

vii   relatively cheap limited editions prints.

viii artists whose work is not often seen by the wider public.

QUESTIONS 10–13

Do the following statements agree with the information given in Reading passage 1? Write:

TRUE   *if the statement agrees with the information*
FALSE   *if the statement contradicts the information*
NOT GIVEN   *if there is no information on this in the passage*

10 Picasso, Warhol, Matisse, Miró and Steinlen are big-name artists. _____

11 It is possible to buy a painting by Picasso for less than £5,000. _____

12 Greeting cards can sell for up to £10,000 each. _____

13 It is not worth investing in new artists or markets because there is a great risk of losing all your money. _____

READING PASSAGE 2

You should spend about 20 minutes on **Questions 14–27** which are based on Reading Passage 2 below:

A

The race to reach 33 miners entombed for 64 days 700m (2,300ft) below the bare brown mountains of the Atacama Desert in Chile could be completed as early as tonight. The chief engineer said this afternoon that within 24 hours the chamber will have been reached. He added that bringing the miners out could begin in three days' time. Three giant drills were boring rescue shafts down through the layers of rock, Laurence Golborne, the Mining Minister, had announced yesterday. How quickly the miners can be extracted once the shafts have reached the men depends on a careful inspection of the shaft, 70cm (28in) wide, by video cameras. If the rock walls are deemed stable the miners could be brought out, one by one, within another two or three days. It is estimated that it will take between 36 and 48 hours to bring them all out.

B

The miners have been trapped underground since August 5, more than twice as long as any other known survivor of a mining accident. A stream of rescue vehicles, satellite television trucks and vehicles carrying journalists from around the world are heading up to the shallow bowl in this lunar landscape that will be a centre of attention over the next few days. In the past 48 hours a specially trained 16-man rescue team, three slim metal rescue capsules, a giant crane, winches and much other equipment have been delivered to Camp Esperanza, as the makeshift settlement is known.

C

Once the shaft is safe, two volunteers, a mining expert from Codelco, the state-owned mining conglomerate, and Sergeant Roberto Rios Seguel, 34, a naval medic and commando, will act as human guinea pigs, descending to where the miners are in the Phoenix – a steel capsule specially made by the Chilean Navy and designed by them together with NASA engineers. It has been painted in the red, white, and blue colours of the Chilean flag. The Phoenix is named for the mythical bird that rose from its ashes, and is the biggest of three custom-built capsules that will be used. It weighs 420 kg. Its interior height is 6 feet, 4 inches (1.9 metres). The miners have been restricted to a diet of 2,000 calories a day to ensure that they can fit into the capsule, which is 53cm wide. The capsule has oxygen tanks in the bottom part. It also has a camera, its own lighting system and a sound system. It has two sets of retractable wheels around it, one near the top and one near the bottom, to help it travel up and down the rescue shaft. The roof of the capsule contains LED lights. If something goes wrong during the rescue, the top part of the capsule can be released and the bottom two thirds of the capsule would then be lowered back down. Should the capsule become jammed, the occupant can open the escape hatch in the base and go back down the shaft.

D

The capsule will be lowered by a large crane at a speed of up to 3ft (91cm) per second. The miners will be wearing a suit with a harness over it, which will allow them to be strapped to the centre of the cylinder in an upright position for the estimated twenty-minute journey to the surface. They will also wear an oxygen mask, a pair of dark glasses to protect their eyes from exposure to the desert sunlight, and a helmet which is specially adapted with a microphone and a wired headset to enable them to communicate with the surface. Doctors will monitor the miners' vital signs using information gathered from a biometric belt. They will conduct a preliminary assessment of the miners' mental and physical health. The miners will then be divided into three groups. The strongest will be the first to make the hazardous ascent to freedom, in case the capsule hits problems, then the weakest. They will be winched up one by one in the slender capsule, rising at just under a metre a second, meaning that each ascent will take about 15 minutes. The entire rescue is expected to take 30 to 40 hours.

E

As each man finally emerges, he will be taken to the nearby field hospital wearing Californian-made sunglasses that filter out all UV rays to protect his eyes. There the men will be given a thorough check-up and, if strong enough, they will be allowed to meet three relatives designated in advance. The miners will then be flown by helicopter to the hospital in Copiapó, where a whole floor has been set aside for them. They are expected to remain there for at least two days.

QUESTIONS 14–15

Reading Passage 2 has five paragraphs **A–E**. Which paragraphs state the following information? Write the appropriate letters **A–E**.

NB There are more paragraphs than summaries, so you will not use them all.

14 The miners' situation is of global interest. _____

15 The length of the operation will be determined by the stability of the physical environment. _____

QUESTIONS 16–20

Complete the summary below.

Choose your answers from the box below the summary and write them into spaces 16-20. You can only use each answer once.

NB There are more words than spaces so you will not use them all.

However, if all goes well, they could be **16** _____ by **17** _____ emergency workers in the next few days. Preparations are already under way. As soon as the miners have been **18** _____, the real rescue operation can start: a specially **19** _____ capsule will be sent down to retrieve them one by one. It is **20** _____ that bringing all of the men back up will take up to forty hours.

trapped	made safe	designed	estimated
trained	freed	completed	known
reached	guessed	carried	restricted

QUESTIONS 21–26

Use *NO MORE THAN THREE WORDS* from the passage to complete each blank in the diagram below.

The Phoenix

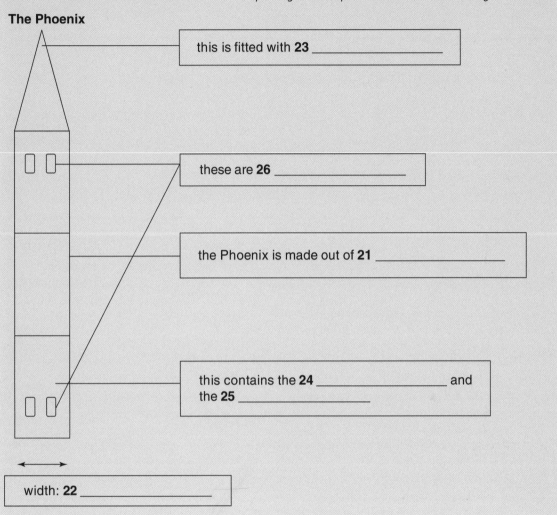

this is fitted with **23** _____

these are **26** _____

the Phoenix is made out of **21** _____

this contains the **24** _____ and the **25** _____

width: **22** _____

QUESTION 27

From the list below, choose the most suitable title for the whole of Reading Passage 2. Write the appropriate letter *A–D*.

A Mine rescue on verge of breakthrough

B Journalists and rescuers race to Chile

C Engineers save the day

D The Phoenix will rise

_____

READING PASSAGE 3

*You should spend about 20 minutes on **Questions 28–40** which are based on Reading Passage 3 below:*

High-tech crime-fighting tools

A

Crime-fighting technology is getting more sophisticated and rightly so. The police need to be equipped for the 21st century. In Britain we've already got the world's biggest DNA database. By next year the state will have access to the genetic data of 4.25m people: one British-based person in 14. Hundreds of thousands of those on the database will never have been charged with a crime.

B

Britain is also reported to have more than 4 million CCTV (closed circuit television) cameras. There is a continuing debate about the effectiveness of CCTV. Some evidence suggests that it is helpful in reducing shoplifting and car crime. It has also been used to successfully identify terrorists and murderers. However, many claim that better lighting is just as effective to prevent crime and that cameras could displace crime. An internal police report said that only one crime was solved for every 1,000 cameras in London in 2007. In short, there is conflicting evidence about the effectiveness of cameras, so it is likely that the debate will continue.

C

Professor Mike Press, who has spent the past decade studying how design can contribute to crime reduction, said that, in order for CCTV to have any effect, it must be used in a targeted way. For example, a scheme in Manchester records every licence plate at the entrance of a shopping complex and alerts police when one is found to belong to an untaxed or stolen car. This is an effective example of monitoring, he said. Most schemes that simply record city centres continually – often not being watched – do not produce results. CCTV can also have the opposite effect of that intended, by giving citizens a false sense of security and encouraging them to be careless with property and personal safety. Professor Press said: 'All the evidence suggests that CCTV alone makes no positive impact on crime reduction and prevention at all. The weight of evidence would suggest the investment is more or less a waste of money unless you have lots of other things in place.' He believes that much of the increase is driven by the marketing efforts of security companies who promote the crime-reducing benefits of their products. He described it as a 'lazy approach to crime prevention' and said that authorities should instead be focusing on how to alter the environment to reduce crime.

D

But in reality, this is not what is happening. Instead, police are considering using more technology. Police forces have recently begun experimenting with cameras in their helmets. The footage will be stored on police computers, along with the footage from thousands of CCTV cameras and millions of pictures from numberplate recognition cameras used increasingly to check up on motorists.

E

And now another type of technology is being introduced. It's called the Microdrone and it's a toy-sized remote-control craft that hovers above streets or crowds to film what's going on beneath. The Microdrone has already been used to monitor rock festivals, but its supplier has also been in discussions to supply it to the Metropolitan Police, and Soca, the Serious Organised Crime Agency. The drones are small enough to be unnoticed by people on the ground when they are flying at 350ft. They contain high-resolution video surveillance equipment and an infrared night vision capability, so even in darkness they give their operators a bird's-eye view of locations while remaining virtually undetectable.

F

The worrying thing is, who will get access to this technology? Merseyside police are already employing two of the devices as part of a pilot scheme to watch football crowds and city parks looking for antisocial behaviour. It is not just about crime detection: West Midlands fire brigade is about to lease a drone, for example, to get a better view of fire and flood scenes and aid rescue attempts; the Environment Agency is considering their use for monitoring of illegal fly tipping and oil spills. The company that makes the drone says it has no plans to license the equipment to individuals or private companies, which hopefully will prevent private security firms from getting their hands on them. But what about local authorities? In theory, this technology could be used against motorists. And where will the surveillance society end? Already there are plans to introduce 'smart water' containing a unique DNA code identifier that when sprayed on a suspect will cling to their clothes and skin and allow officers to identify them later. As long as high-tech tools are being used in the fight against crime and terrorism, fine. But if it's another weapon to be used to invade our privacy then we don't want it.

Glossary:
drone: a remote-controlled pilotless aircraft
350ft: about 107 meters
bird's eye view: a view from above
fly-tipping: illegally dumping waste (British English)

Answer key

1 Family matters

Part 1: Vocabulary

Exercise 1

1 friend: someone who you know well and like, but who is not related to you
  mate: friend; someone's wife, husband, or sexual partner
  flatmate: a person who shares a flat with someone
2 sister: a girl or woman who has the same parents as you
  sister-in-law: the sister of your husband or wife, or the woman who is married to your brother
3 brother: a boy or man who has the same parents as you
  sister: a girl or woman who has the same parents as you
  sibling: your brother or sister
4 boyfriend: a man or boy with whom someone is having a romantic or sexual relationship
  husband: the man a woman is married to
  partner: the person someone is married to or is having a romantic or sexual relationship with
5 colleague: a person you work with, especially in a professional job
  business partner: the person with whom you share the ownership of a firm or business
6 acquaintance: someone who you have met and know slightly, but not well
  stranger: someone you have never met before
7 aunt: the sister of your mother or father, or the wife of your uncle
  great-aunt: the aunt of one of your parents
8 half-sister: a girl or woman who has either the same mother or the same father as you
  step-sister: the daughter of the man or woman who has married one of your parents after the death of the other parent, or after a divorce

Exercise 2

1 d, 2 e, 3 a, 4 f, c, b

Exercise 3

<u>Widows</u> and <u>widowers</u> whose <u>spouses</u> pass away ... If a person dies ... his or her <u>spouse</u> or <u>civil partner</u> is changing from £125,000 to £250,000 where there are <u>children</u>.
Experts have welcomed the change, ... if you are <u>unmarried</u> or <u>separated</u> but not <u>divorced</u>. However, people should not be misled ... <u>unmarried couples</u> are not entitled ... their <u>other half</u> ...
  <u>Modern family life</u> is becoming ... <u>second marriages</u> and <u>children</u> from more than one <u>relationship</u>. A will is the only way to ensure that <u>those you love or are obliged to care for</u> are adequately provided for.
  After the <u>spouse</u> has received his or her legal share, the rest of the estate is shared by <u>children</u> or <u>grandchildren</u>. If there are none, surviving <u>parents</u> will get a share. If there are none of these, any <u>brothers</u> and <u>sisters</u> who shared the same two <u>parents</u> as the deceased will receive a share.
  If your <u>family circumstances</u> have changed, ... For example, you may be <u>separated</u> and your <u>ex-partner</u> now lives with someone else. If you are <u>married</u> or enter into <u>a registered civil partnership</u>, this will invalidate any previous will you have made.

Exercise 4

1 f, 2 h, 3 a, 4 i, 5 g, 6 b, 7 c, 8 j, 9 d, 10 l, 11 e, 12 k

Part 2:   Practice exercises

Exercise 1
Suggested answer:
The paragraph is about family celebrations and gives advice about how parents and their grown-up children should behave when they are together.

Exercise 2
Paragraph a
1 The first sentence is the topic sentence: it informs readers that the paragraph is about a report, and refers to the subject of the report.
2 It becomes more specific. This is often the case in texts: the writer starts by introducing a topic in general terms, and then gives more detailed information.
3 'The break-up' refers to what was mentioned previously: 'separation or divorce'. 'The' is often used for information that has been mentioned before, whereas 'a' is often used for new information. This demonstrates how grammar can sometimes help you work out meaning.

Paragraph b
4 Yes. If we do not underestimate something, we give it its rightful value.
5 The first and last sentences express the same idea. In this case, we could say that the last sentence explains the first sentence. This is quite common in paragraphs: the first sentence introduces the topic and the last one summarises the topic.
6 The first sentence is the topic sentence.

Paragraph c
7 The first sentence is the introduction, the last one is the conclusion, and the two in the middle make up the main body.
8 The introduction. Even without the rest of the paragraph, we would understand what the writer is trying to say. That is not true for any of the other sentences. Note: The main body gives more specific information, and explains what the anti-discrimination laws would mean. The conclusion says what the consequences of these laws would be.
9 'Friendly' here means 'kind to', 'making it easier for', 'making it better for'.

Exercise 3
1 c
cause: anti-discrimination laws (e.g. parenting as a school subject, rebuilt staircases, forbidding advertising for certain products, new work regulations)
effect: a family-friendly society, less divorce and crime, earning less, producing less
2 b
conclusion: grandparents are of great value to their grandchildren
supporting evidence: the report, the fact that in difficult times children need someone who can be calm, e.g. a grandparent
3 a
This paragraph describes what can happen after a separation or divorce: grandparents don't see their grandchildren or cannot provide childcare anymore.

Exercise 4
Suggested answers:
1 The traditional family unit
2 The advantages and disadvantages of traditional families
3 Advice for sleepovers
Note: You did not need to read the second paragraph completely in order to write a heading. It was clearly divided into two main points.

Exercise 5
Section a: ix *(Families function as the cornerstone of society, taking care of social organization and of socializing children.)*
Section b: viii *(The family was on the whole seen as important: it was adapted to the needs of society and also met the needs of the family itself.)*
Section c: v *(Writers wrote about the disadvantages of the traditional model and society started to have fewer traditional families.)* Note: Heading vii *(the first criticisms of family)* is only part of the issue.
Section d: i *(This section discusses the point of view of people who see new models as positive (welcomed ... choice), and those who see them as negative (instability, insecurity)).*
Section e: ii *(Politicians have spoken about families and have made policies.)*
Note: Heading ix could relate to the whole article, but not to one particular section of it.

Part 3: Exam practice

Section A: i ('Science' relates to 'studies', 'research', 'analysis' and 'data'. Note that this paragraph mentions modern technology (v), but that is not the main idea in the paragraph.)
Section B: ii (The main idea of the paragraph is in the last sentence. 'Honest communication' relates to 'talking about problems and working through them'. This is 'important', as not being honest about problems and 'keeping the peace' can have negative consequences: 'harmful effects on a relationship'. Note that this paragraph mentions avoiding arguments (vi), but this is described as harmful, not a benefit.)
Section C: iii (Certain thoughts can be 'powerful' because they have the ability to eventually end relationships: 'once the idea of divorce is in somebody's mind, they are more likely to act on it'. Note that this paragraph mentions marrying again (iv), 'remarriage' but does not talk about the likelihood of this happening.)
Section D: viii ('Early' refers to 'at the beginning of their marriage', 'dissatisfaction' refers to 'disappointed' and 'consequences' refers to 'divorce'.)
Section E: vii (The previous paragraph suggested that early disappointment is a predictor for divorce, whereas this paragraph suggests that, in truth, the 'real' predictor is 'the result of a combination of small incidents that add up over time'. Conversely, a 'lasting' or 'happy' marriage lies in 'the effort made on a daily basis by both partners'.)

2 Healthcare

Part 1: Vocabulary

Exercise 1
a 2, b 5, c 3, d 1, e 6, f 4

Exercise 2
1 f, 2 e, 3 a, 4 c, 5 d, 6 b

Exercise 3
1 b, 2 a, 3 a

Exercise 4
1 fatalities: deaths (synonym)
2 scalded: burnt (synonym)
3 kit: equipment (synonym)
4 ignorance: knowledge (or common sense) (antonym)

Exercise 5
1 to commission, 2 a survey, 3 to recover, 4 an injury, 5 to equip, 6 aid, 7 to ignore

Part 2: Practice exercises

Exercise 1
1 Report on Social Insurance,　2 1942,　3 social insurance,　4 five/5
5 Want, Disease, Ignorance, Squalor, Idleness,　6 poor housing and homelessness,
7 the existence of poverty in Britain

Exercise 2
State responsibility:
- community provision in some societies, e.g. in Israeli kibbutzim
- in England, some involvement in caring for the poor since Elizabethan times: 1601 Poor Law (money was collected from each household and given to the needy)

Support from the church: provided charitable support when the state didn't

Exercise 3
Paragraph 2: This gives examples of how and by whom vulnerable people are supported in different societies and discusses attitudes to the vulnerable.
Paragraph 3: This discusses the support given to the vulnerable in England since the seventeenth century.
Notice how this passage moves from the general to the specific: introduction of topic, the vulnerable in different societies, the vulnerable in England.

Exercise 4
1 Paragraph 2 (*In some societies, the care of the vulnerable is seen as the responsibility of the family or the village* and *Attitudes to the vulnerable vary.*)
2 Paragraph 1 (*In all societies there are groups of people who are potentially vulnerable. These include children, older people, people with disabilities, and the poor, for example.*)
3 Paragraph 3 (*Not until the opening years of the twentieth century did the state begin to take a proactive role in the care and welfare of its citizens.*)
4 Paragraph 2 (*In some societies, the care of the vulnerable is seen as the responsibility of the family or the village. In others, it is principally the responsibility of the state, through community provision.*)

Exercise 5
1 shapes,　2 heights,　3 physical abilities,　4 genes,　5 ageing,　6 diets,
7 general quality of life

Check that you have used no more than four words for each answer.

Exercise 6
2 children under 15, but not the first child
3 The National Insurance Act 1946
4 all workers who paid weekly from their wages into the national insurance scheme
5 The National Assistance Act 1948
6 a minimum income
7 The National Health Service Act 1948
8 the whole national population
Note: The clear organisation of a text can help you. Each paragraph normally makes a separate point and here there is a clear division between the different Acts, which helps you to find the rest of the information that you are looking for. In some cases the information from the text needs to be re-organised: the National Health Service Act mentions three principles but in the table there is a separate section for information about who the payment is for (see number 8).

Part 3: Exam practice

1 £30, 2 £80, 3 £3.70, 4 599.3 / almost 600, 5 288.3, 6 267

Notes:
- This is a long text, so it is important that you do not read all of it. You are not expected to demonstrate your understanding of the text but your ability to find specific information in it.
- You are asked for very specific information and this is not usually found in the first paragraph.
- Most of the missing information consists of numbers, so scanning is a good technique to use. Scanning for the names of the drugs is also helpful.
- The example that was already filled in (458) should alert you to the fact that you do not need to write '£' or 'million'; that information is already given in the heading.

3   Getting an education

Part 1:   Vocabulary

Exercise 1
a 2,   b 3,   c 4,   d 6,   e 5,   f 1

Exercise 2
1 d,   2 e,   3 a,   4 f,   5 c,   6 g,   7 b

Exercise 3
If you send your child to a <u>boarding school</u> you can be looking at <u>fees</u> of almost £8,000 per <u>term</u>. Eton will charge £7,896 a term from September — a rise of 5.8% on last year's fees. Winchester's fees have gone up 5% from £7,457 to £7,833 a term. <u>Day schools</u> are cheaper, but even these are charging an average of £2,796 a term — £8,388 a year.

If you have a baby this year and plan to send him or her to a <u>private day school</u> for <u>secondary education</u>, it will set you back about £150,000, according to an independent adviser.

If your child is starting <u>senior school</u> this September, the school fees between 11 and 18 will total an average of £75,500, assuming the fees rise by 7% a year.

Exercise 4
1 h,   2 f,   3 j,   4 c,   5 a,   6 g,   7 i,   8 b,   9 d,   10 e

Notes:
- In Britain, a public school is a private independent secondary school. It is fee-paying and normally a boarding school. In the United States, a public school is a school supported by public funds.
- primary school (Britain) = elementary school (USA)

Exercise 5
4 General Certificate of Secondary Education

Exercise 6
1 a (The meaning must be negative: the mother says she felt 'like a monster'.)

2 c (The authority wants to do something contrary to what the experts say and parents want, so the answer cannot be 'b', which mentions agreement. The image of a wall as an obstacle might help you work out the meaning.)

3 a ('unable to cope' and 'struggling to get his needs met' suggest that this is an illness or condition. 'Cater' does not relate to food here, but the ability to meet other types of needs.)

4 b (The word 'progress' ('it's worth it to see Joshua making progress') should give you the answer.)

5 b (The meaning must be positive: the school 'passed' the inspection. 'Satisfactory' is not strong enough, and 'with an intense colour and shine' does not make sense in relation to the word 'report'.)

6 c (The meaning must be negative: 'face years of fighting'. It must also express this idea with a degree of intensity: 'a terrible blow'.)

Exercise 7
1 assuming,   2 to rise,   3 expertise,   4 youngster,   5 progress,   6 inspection,   7 diagnosis, 8 realisation

---

Part 2:   Practice exercises

Exercise 1
1 6,   2 20,   3 11,   4 6

Exercise 2
(Possible answers)
1 By bicycle./ I walked.
2 No, I don't. / Mrs Findleton.
3 English, French, History. / The 3 sciences.
4 Getting the giggles. / Winning a prize.
5 Failing Chemistry. / Breaking my leg.
6 Mostly sandwiches. / Rice and vegetables.
7 Yes, Geography. / No, never.
8 Nothing. / Engineering.

Exercise 3
The order is 2, 1, 4, 3.
Policies can be influenced by many forces. For example, (2) Jamie Oliver's TV programme, *Jamie's School Dinners*, attacking the quality of food in schools, eventually persuaded the Minister for Education to rethink policies about the eating habits of children, (1) as well as budgets. Equally so, (4) very large organisations with a global presence influence policy makers all around the world over concerns (3) such as oil, arms, the environment and human rights.

Exercise 4
Paragraph 1: Introduction of the plans
Paragraph 2: More background and some details
Paragraph 3: The reaction of the National Union of Students
Paragraph 4: Detailed information about the review recommendations
Paragraph 5: The reaction of universities
Paragraph 6: The reaction of unions and newer universities
Paragraph 7: Defence of the plans

Exercise 5
Strategies 2 and 6 (in that order) are very useful.
Strategies 1 and 3 are time-consuming and not really relevant.
Strategy 5 is pointless.
Strategy 4 might be useful, but underlining the key words is better.

Exercise 6
Suggested answers:
1 Who is against the proposed changes to student tuition fees?
2 How could a future loan repayment schedule be described in comparison to today's?

3 According to the <u>official</u> statement from the National Union of Students, <u>who</u> will <u>suffer</u> <u>financially</u>?
4 From the point of <u>view</u> of <u>students</u>, <u>what</u> would be the <u>negative consequences</u> of <u>higher</u> tuition <u>fees</u>?
5 In the future, <u>what</u> <u>may become</u> the <u>deciding factor</u> for students <u>choosing</u> a <u>university</u>?
6 <u>What</u> will <u>happen</u> to the <u>maximum</u> period of <u>repayment</u>?
7 <u>What</u> will <u>students</u> whose <u>parents</u> earn a <u>total of £55,000</u> receive?
8 According to <u>Universities UK</u>, <u>who</u> would <u>especially</u> <u>benefit</u> from the new system?
9 According to <u>newer</u> <u>universities</u>, <u>what</u> might <u>happen</u> to the <u>number</u> of <u>people</u> who are <u>able</u> to <u>move up in society</u>?
10 <u>Who</u> may <u>ask</u> for fees of <u>over £7,000</u>?

Exercise 7

1 students and lecturers *(Plans to allow universities to charge unlimited tuition fees were today greeted with dismay from <u>students and lecturers</u>)*
2 later and longer (Graduates would also repay their loans <u>later</u> and over a <u>longer</u> period.)
3 the next generation *(Lord Browne's review would ... force <u>the next generation</u> to pick up the tab for devastating cuts to higher education)*
4 higher debts *(The only thing students and their families would stand to gain from higher fees would be <u>higher debts</u>.)*
5 cost (A market in course prices between universities would increasingly put pressure on students to make decisions <u>based on cost</u>)
6 a five-year extension *(Student loans would be paid over a maximum of <u>30 years</u> ... The current maximum is <u>25 years</u>.)*
7 partial grants *(Full grants would go to students whose family income was £25,000 or less and <u>partial grants</u> to those with <u>household income up to £60,000</u>.)*
8 disadvantaged students *(This will be crucial in supporting <u>those from disadvantaged backgrounds</u> through university.)*
9 a large decrease *(There is a real risk that some students who would have gone to university will <u>decide not to go</u> and that opportunity and <u>social mobility will be fatally undermined</u>.)*
10 some top universities *(with many research universities likely to charge <u>£6,000 or £7,000 a year, a handful of top universities charging higher fees</u>)*

Note: Always check that you have not used too many words.

Exercise 8
Suggested answers:
2 loans and jobs,   3 a press release,   4 possible overtiredness,   5 close to university,
6 a four-year course,   7 location, cost, results,   8 a personal approach,   9 social skill development,
10 possession of mobiles

Note: Did you write a maximum of three words for each answer?

Exercise 9
Suggested answers:
1 college communication changes,   2 timetable information corrections,   3 time-saving methods,   4 more book loans,   5 term-time drama productions ('plays' refers to theatrical productions, i.e. 'drama'),   6 after-school sports activities,   7 resource management,
8 student satisfaction

Part 3: Exam practice

1 to keep employees *(Children's centres are offering up to £7,000 a year more for managers and nursery nurses to staff their premises, forcing private providers to match the pay offer or risk losing their best employees.)*
2 £17,000 *(Senior nursery nurses ... could still earn up to £17,000 if they switched to a children's centre.)*

3 78 per cent (*Private providers currently account for 78 per cent of all nursery places.*)
4 private and voluntary (*Parents have also made clear during public consultations that they like private and voluntary sector nurseries*)

4 Water

Part 1: Vocabulary

Exercise 1
a 6, b 3, c 5, d 1, e 2, f 4

Exercise 2
1 h, 2 j, 3 i, 4 a, 5 f, 6 c, 7 b, 8 e, 9 d, 10 g

Exercise 3
1 c, 2 g, 3 a, 4 d, 5 b, 6 e, 7 f

Exercise 4
Make a couple of <u>litres</u> of <u>stock</u> from the vegetables. Meanwhile, <u>boil</u> the <u>kettle</u> again and <u>pour</u> the <u>boiling water</u> on the spinach. Then turn up the heat in the pan with the onions, add the rice and toast lightly. Add boiling <u>stock spoon</u> by spoon to the rice. After 15 minutes of gentle <u>simmering</u>, <u>spoon</u> the risotto onto the plates and put a <u>runny</u> fried egg and the spinach on top.

With dessert, pour each person a <u>glass</u> of sweet white <u>wine</u>. Cut a slice of peach into each glass, so that you roll fruit and wine together into your mouth – a simple way to end this meal.

Exercise 5
1 a, 2 f, 3 g, 4 e, 5 c, 6 d, 7 b

Exercise 6
Suggested answers:
Water: boating, diving, jet-skiing, rowing, sailing, scuba diving, snorkelling, surfing, swimming, water polo, water-skiing
Ice: curling, figure skating, ice-climbing, ice hockey, luge, speed-skating
Snow: ski jumping, skiing (alpine skiing, cross-country skiing), snow blading, snowboarding

Exercise 7
1 meanders, 2 gushed, 3 poured, 4 trickling, 5 seeping, 6 flowed

Part 2: Practice exercises

Exercise 1
Suggested answers:
1 noun / noun phrase / gerund (*Small and medium-sized enterprises (SMEs) are responsible **for*** (preposition); therefore what follows must be a noun, noun phrase, or gerund, e.g. *responsible for <u>the environment</u> / <u>paying</u> their taxes.*)
2 noun / noun phrase / gerund (*Between 70 and 75 per cent of SMEs are unaware **of*** (preposition); therefore what follows must be a noun, noun phrase or gerund, e.g. *unaware of <u>the tax benefits</u> / <u>the problems they face.</u>*)
3 linking word + noun / linking word + clause (*Unfortunately a lot of small companies don't think about the environment* could be a complete sentence; therefore what follows is most probably a

linking word of some kind, e.g. *don't think about the environment or their responsibilities / and are unaware of their responsibilities / which is regrettable*.)

4 preposition (*In 1994 just 20 per cent of businesses in the UK accepted the link + between* (+ noun). The noun *link* is usually followed by the preposition *between*, e.g. *the link between these two issues*).

5 preposition / linking word + clause (e.g. *a further £3 billion in costs / if they made the effort*).

Exercise 2
1 d,   2 c,   3 f,   4 b,   5 a,   6 g,   7 e,   8 h

Exercise 3
The order is: 3, 2, 4, 1.

Small and medium-sized enterprises (SMEs) are responsible for up to 80 per cent of environmental crimes and more than 60 per cent of the commercial and industrial waste produced in England and Wales, according to research by the Environment Agency. The body says, however, that between 70 and 75 per cent of SMEs are unaware of their environmental obligations. Many SMEs also believe that (3) environmental compliance would be too costly and the benefits limited. (2) Only few businesses realise how much energy spending could be reduced by doing something simple such as switching off machines that are not in use.

(4) While a fundamental shift in business attitudes is desired, agencies like Envirowise are aware that profit incentives may instead be the answer. For instance, Westbury Dairies, in Wiltshire, has introduced a system to collect and reuse condensation formed during the milk evaporation process. This has reduced the demand for mains water by about 90 per cent. Cost savings from purchasing water alone exceed £340,000 per year. But businesses like Westbury Dairies are still in the minority. It is estimated that (1) UK businesses could save a further £3 billion through improved environmental performance.

Exercise 4
Suggested answers:
1 Searching for artefacts under the sea ...
2 The sea, like space, is ...
3 Complex survival equipment must ...
4 The alternative to diving suits and air tanks is ...
5 The expedition was a cover story ...
6 One of the most important things that an archaeologist will need in searching the seabed is ...
7 Sonar is a tried and tested technology ...
8 Even more problematic than recovering artefacts is ...

Exercise 5
1 c (*One of the most important things that an archaeologist will need ... is solid research. Academics and treasure hunters can spend years studying old documents for clues of where best to begin.*)
Incorrect answers:
a: 'hard work on some occasions' does not mean 'some of the most difficult work'.
b: 'an alien environment' refers to the sea, not finding items.
d: Although common sense dictates that '*good diving skills*' may be required, the information is not in the text itself.

2 c (*Even more problematic than recovering artefacts is preserving them*)
Incorrect answers:
a: Sonar technology is not new, it is 'tried and tested'.
b: The text does not say that finding artefacts was very successful in the sixties; it says sonar was used successfully in the sixties, i.e. it worked.
d: William Kidd's ship is one of the finds, but the text does not say what William Kidd himself did.

Exercise 6

1 a (b is factually incorrect. It suggests that more than one newspaper said this; there was no mention of a large number of passengers, just that passengers in general dislike tipping more and more.)

2 a (b uses synonyms, e.g. 'larger' for 'more', and 'adaptation' for 'major change' but this is not done well: 'larger' does not mean 'more' in this context, and 'big adaptation' is not a good collocation.)

3 b (a mentions 'accusation', which is not the same as an 'implication'.)

Exercise 7

a Paragraphs: 6, 7
b Paragraphs: 3, 4, 5, 7
c Paragraphs: 1, 2, 3, 5, 8, 9
d Paragraphs: 1, 2

Exercise 8

1 a ('The future of the UK's coastal cities is in jeopardy due to rising sea levels,' reported Lloyd's. Similarly, nine out of the world's ten largest cities are located on low-lying coastal land.)

2 d (dragging people onto big waves with jet skis or even helicopters)

3 c (the existence of freak waves was confirmed in 1995 in Norway, where an 84-foot wave occurred)

4 b (it's useful to distinguish between tsunamis, which are caused by geological events (such as landslides or earthquakes))

5 – (It is popular with one TV presenter, Laird Hamilton, but 'presenters' implies many people.)

6 a (As the waters heat up, ... sea levels rise.)

7 c (giant waves ... deposited on New Orleans by Hurricane Katrina)

8 c (For centuries, sailors told of the existence of monstrous waves up to 100f feet high that could appear without warning in mid-ocean, ... often in perfectly clear and calm weather.)

9 c (The fact that ocean waves are getting bigger must be exhilarating for all of them. For the rest of us, however, big waves are very bad news indeed.)

10 c (giant waves generated by weather)

11 b (The Alaskan wave is believed to have been a tsunami, caused by a landslide. It's useful to distinguish between tsunamis, which are caused by geological events (such as landslides or earthquakes))

12 c (enthusiasts who tune into weather reports, and catch the first plane to wherever the big waves are expected to hit land)

Part 3: Exam practice

1
C (Law ... plans to have three wells at the plant) **or**
D (The company has a head start. In 1976, the government-funded Hot Dry Rock Research Project began deep drilling to study the area's geology. Law plans to use the detailed maps the team produced over fifteen years to direct his efforts.)

2
F (the industry has so far failed to demonstrate it can fulfil its promise)

Incorrect answers:
A: 'once renowned' means that it is not famous for that any more.
B: 'It is like someone has put a power station below ground and you are simply tapping into it' means that it is not really like that.
E: It has not always been global, as conventionally, 'it tends to be confined to volcanically active regions or areas close to fault lines'. Also, 'Law claims the process his company uses removes this limitation, making the industry viable almost anywhere in the world.' He claims that it is will be possible in the future.

Note: Pay attention to punctuation:
- 'Geothermal Engineering' is written with initial capital letters. This is because it is the name of a company. However, 'geothermal industry' does not have capital letters and refers to the industry in general, not to a particular company.
- 'Law' is always spelled with capital letters. This is because it is a name. The name 'Law' should not be confused with the word 'law'. It is the name of the director of the company, so Law's views represent the company's views.

Pay attention to grammatical information:

'Law, a former consultant to the geothermal industry, plans to have three wells at the plant': the commas tell you that 'Law' is 'a former consultant to the geothermal industry'. It is not the industry that is planning the wells; it is Law, the founder of Geothermal Engineering.

5   Non-verbal clues

Part 1:   Vocabulary

Exercise 1
a 2,   b 1,   c 3,   d 6,   e 4,   f 5

Exercise 2
Suggested answers:

Poor <u>communication</u> between NHS hospitals and care homes may be putting elderly people at risk of contracting MRSA and other infections, the health and social care regulator has <u>warned</u>. The Care Quality Commission (CQC) found nearly one in five homes in England were not <u>being told</u> if patients discharged from hospitals were or had been infected.

Hospitals are meant to include a <u>written</u> infection <u>history</u> on discharge <u>summaries</u>. But the <u>survey revealed</u> 17 per cent of care homes <u>said</u> they did not <u>receive information</u> from hospitals, while another 28 per cent complained of incomplete and <u>illegible data.</u>

Ambulance crews were also often left <u>uninformed</u>. Where there was communication about patients, it was <u>verbal</u> and not <u>written down</u>. A <u>spokesperson</u> said: 'If we are to tackle infections effectively we need to check that all providers of care are <u>talking to each other.</u>'

Exercise 3
1 smiling,   2 shake/shaking,   3 wave,   4 nudges,   5 nod,   6 clapping,   7 shrugged,
8 winked,   9 Pointing,   10 frowning

Exercise 4
1 P,   2 N,   3 N,   4 P,   5 P,   6 P,   7 N,   8 N

Exercise 5
1 e,   2 d,   3 a,   4 f,   5 c,   6 g,   7 b

Part 2:   Practice exercises

Exercise 1
Check that you have chosen the correct number of options.

Exercise 2
The right order is 3, 1, 4, 2.
1: second paragraph,   2: fourth paragraph,   3: first paragraph,   4: third paragraph

Exercise 3
Suggested answers:
1 <u>Why</u> has it always been <u>difficult</u> to <u>test</u> the idea of a <u>connection</u> between <u>our taste</u> for <u>music</u> and the <u>calls</u> of <u>monkeys</u>?
2 <u>What</u> do <u>monkeys prefer</u>: <u>music</u> or <u>silence</u>?
3 Is it <u>true</u> that monkeys <u>appeared</u> to be <u>calmed down</u> by listening to the <u>heavy metal band Metallica</u>?
4 <u>Who suggested</u> this <u>new</u> kind of <u>experiment</u> to Professor <u>Snowdon</u>?

Exercise 4
Your summaries will be different from the ones below, but compare them to see if you were on the right track.
1 Monkeys normally like silence more than any kind of music, although in one case they seemed to relax when they heard music by Metallica.
2 However, Charles Snowdon has shown that one particular species of monkey is affected when they hear music that is written specifically for them, even though they do not react to ordinary music.
3 The research indicates that people may have inherited their enjoyment of music from the ancestors they have in common with monkeys.
4 David Teie, a colleague of Professor Snowdon's, suggested the new method to him.

Exercise 5
Suggested answers:
1 <u>What</u> made the <u>sounds</u> on the <u>recorded song</u> for the <u>monkeys</u> in the experiment?
  • the cello
  • the human voice
2 <u>What behaviour</u> did the <u>monkeys</u> display when they were played the '<u>threat' song</u>?
  • they moved around more
  • they showed more anxious and social behaviour
  • they sometimes faced towards the hidden speaker
3 <u>What happened</u> when the <u>monkeys</u> were played a <u>calming song</u>?
  • they moved less
  • they showed calmer and less social behaviour
  • there was increased feeding

Exercise 6
Your answers will be different, but compare them to the following to see if you were on the right track:
1 <u>What</u> is <u>innovative</u> about the <u>predictive texting system</u> that has been <u>developed</u> by Sanjay <u>Patel</u>?
  The software recognises the way individual users write and can predict what words they will write next, so fewer keystrokes are needed.
2 What <u>types</u> of <u>hardware</u> and <u>software</u> could work <u>differently</u> in the <u>future because</u> of this <u>invention</u>?
  Mobile phones and computers; e-mail, text messaging and word-processing.
3 What <u>characteristics</u> of the <u>new systems</u> make them so <u>fascinating</u> for the <u>general public</u>?
  Technology like computers and mobile phones will be easier to use and the software will function unobtrusively.
4 <u>Why</u> is this <u>invention important</u> for <u>Scotland</u>?
  He has received support from Scottish organisations and is based in Scotland so they are a part of his success.

Exercise 7

1 d *(the software application... is set to change the way we punch information into our mobile phones and computer keyboards)*

Incorrect answers:

a: This is true but it is not what makes it innovative.

b: The opposite is true: it learns to recognise patterns.

c: This may be true but the text does not say or imply that this is what makes it innovative.

2 a (These are all mentioned in the text and are examples of both software and hardware.)

Incorrect answers:

b: Adaptex is the name of the new system itself.

c: These are mentioned but the answer is not as complete as 'a'.

d: These are not examples of hardware and software.

3 b *('We don't want to change people's practices, we have to complement or improve them. But you can't expect people to change unless you make things better, simpler to use and non-intrusive. I think that's why AdapTex intelligence systems are creating such interest.')*

Incorrect answers:

a: There is no mention of a complete change; the text simply says that people will be able to input information more quickly.

c and d: These are true but they are not what makes the system fascinating for the general public.

4 d (Sanjay has received support from Scottish organisations and now lives in Scotland so the country shares in his success.)

Incorrect answers:

a and b: These are true, but the link with his success is not as clear as it is in 'd'.

c: There is no connection to Scotland in this answer.

Exercise 8

1 b *(Sanjay, now 38)*

d *(Over the past 15 years, Patel has worked within systems architecture in telecoms and finance.)*

Incorrect answers:

a: He has a brother, but we do not know if he has only one.

c: His nationality is not mentioned.

e: We know that he worked under the guidance of the Chicago Board of Trade and completed his two-year contract in a little over a year. That is not the same as saying that he worked in Chicago for 2 years.

2 a *(Today Sanjay Patel lives in Partick in Glasgow.)*

b *(Today Sanjay Patel lives in Partick in Glasgow. Previously from Croydon, he was encouraged to move to Scotland)*

f *(He is delighted with the support he has been given in Scotland.)*

Incorrect answers:

c and d: There is no evidence for this in the text.

e: *He was brought up in London*

Part 3: Exam practice

1 B *('What our discovery showed is that the alarm calls were far more complex than we had thought,' said Zuberbühler. 'They were conveying information that was contextual, self-aware and intelligent.'* The explanation of 'far more complex' comes in the next sentence: 'conveying information that was contextual, self-aware and intelligent'.)

Incorrect answers:

A: The text says that animals also use complex communication *(proof that the ability to construct a complex form of communication is not unique to man).*

C: The text says that there is communication across species but this is not a definition of 'complex information'.

D: The opposite is true: the text says that these monkeys can understand the complex alarm calls.

2 B (Researchers taught some chimpanzees to hold conversations; one chimp had a vocabulary of 3,000 words and the language skills of a four-year-old child.)

Incorrect answers:

A: The text mentions intelligence in chimpanzees and birds but does not compare them to each other.

C: The text says that the chimpanzees at Georgia State University can use keyboards to communicate; this is not the same as saying they can play the keyboard, which means they can be taught to play music.

D: The text says that one chimpanzee might have the language skills of a four-year old child but there is no suggestion that all chimpanzees have those skills.

3 A (In an experiment seven crows successfully reeled in a piece of food placed out of reach using three different lengths of stick. Crucially, they were able to complete the task without any special training, suggesting the birds were capable of a level of abstract reasoning and creativity normally associated only with humans.)

Incorrect answers:

B: The text says that the birds were able of a level of reasoning similar to that of humans, not that they could use multiple tools better than humans.

C: The text says that the birds 'were able to read numbers from left to right, as humans do, and count to four even when the line of numbers was moved from vertical to horizontal', but this does not mean they are able to read numbers as well as humans.

D: The opposite is true: they do better at tests when they have slept well: 'birds performed better in tests after a good night's sleep'.

6   Scientists at work

Part 1:   Vocabulary

Exercise 1
a 3,   b 5,   c 6,   d 2,   e 4,   f 1

Exercise 2
-logy: biology, ecology, geology, meteorology, palaeontology, pharmacology, zoology
-metry: geometry, optometry
-graphy: cartography, geography
-ics: acoustics, ballistics, economics, electronics, genetics, mathematics, mechanics, physics, statistics
-ing: computing, engineering
other: anatomy, astronomy, botany, chemistry

Exercise 3
1 b,   2 d,   3 i,   4 g,   5 f,   6 h,   7 c,   8 e,   9 l,   10 j,   11 k,   12 a

Exercise 4
You may have studied some topics at school (e.g. chemistry, geometry (a branch of mathematics), physics, economics, mathematics, biology), and others in higher education (e.g. engineering, zoology, botany).

Exercise 5

1 d, 2 e, 3 a, 4 b, 5 c

Exercise 6

1 a cartographer, 2 a biologist, 3 a geneticist, 4 a botanist, 5 a physicist,
6 a palaeontologist, 7 an ecologist, 8 an astronomer, 9 a geologist

Exercise 7

Last month the Institute of (a) <u>Cell and Molecular Science</u> (ICMS) was opened, giving an insight into the traditionally secret world of the (a) <u>scientist</u>.

When the project was being planned, classes of schoolchildren were asked to describe how they saw scientists. They all gave details of white middle-aged men with glasses and beards. Only one girl chose to describe a female scientist, but even she had a beard. When the children were asked about (a) <u>cells</u>, they thought of prison cells, even battery cells, but never the cells that make up all of us.

Visiting schoolchildren will be able to look down on scientists at work among the (b) <u>test tubes</u>, (b) <u>flasks</u>, (b) <u>microscopes</u> and (b) <u>centrifuges</u> of a state-of-the-art (a) <u>research facility</u>. They can then enter The Centre of the Cell – the (a) 'embryo' pod – where they can learn about the basics of (a) <u>cell biology</u>, (a) <u>disease</u> and (a) <u>genetics</u>. After seeing the scientists at work, children enter the pod where interactive screens will give them a theatrical taste of everything from (a) <u>cell division</u> and (a) <u>tooth decay</u> to (a) <u>cancer</u>, (a) <u>cloning</u> and (a) <u>gene therapy</u>.

Exercise 8

1 giving (give), 2 gave (give), 3 state-of-the-art, 4 decay, 5 therapy

---

Part 2: Practice exercises

Exercise 1

Dolphins have been declared (b) <u>the world's second most intelligent creatures after humans</u>, with scientists suggesting they are (b) <u>so bright that they should be treated as 'non-human persons'</u>.

Studies into dolphin behaviour have highlighted (b) <u>how similar their communications are to those of humans and that they are brighter than chimpanzees</u>. These have been backed up by anatomical research showing that (b) <u>dolphin brains have many key features associated with high intelligence</u>. The researchers argue that their work shows it (b) <u>is morally unacceptable to keep such intelligent animals in amusement parks or to kill them</u> for food or by accident when fishing. Some 300,000 whales, dolphins and porpoises die in this way each year.

(a) '<u>Many dolphin brains are larger than our own and second in mass only to the human brain when corrected for body size</u>,' said Lori Marino, a zoologist at Emory University in Atlanta, Georgia, who has used magnetic (a) <u>resonance imaging scans to map the brains of dolphin species and compare them with those of primates</u>. (a) '<u>The neuroanatomy suggests psychological continuity between humans and dolphins</u> and has profound implications for the ethics of human-dolphin interactions,' she added.

Dolphins have (b) <u>long been recognised as among the most intelligent of animals</u>. Recently, a series of behavioural studies has suggested that dolphins, especially species such as (a) <u>the bottlenose, whose brains weigh about 5lb</u>, (b) <u>could even be brighter than chimps, which some studies have found can reach the intelligence levels of three-year-old children</u>. The studies show how dolphins have distinct personalities, a strong sense of self and (b) <u>can think about the future</u>.

It has also become clear that they are 'cultural' animals, meaning that (b) <u>new types of behaviour can quickly be picked up by one dolphin from another</u>. In one study, Diana Reiss, professor of psychology at Hunter College, City University of New York, showed that (b) <u>bottlenose dolphins could recognise themselves in a mirror and use it to inspect various parts of their bodies</u>, (b) <u>an ability that had been thought limited to humans and great apes</u>. In another, she found that captive animals also had (b) <u>the ability to learn a rudimentary symbol-based language</u>.

Other research has shown (b) <u>dolphins can solve difficult problems</u>, while those living in the wild (b) <u>co-operate in ways that imply complex social structures and a high level of emotional sophistication</u>. In one recent case, a dolphin rescued from the wild was taught to tail-walk while recuperating for three weeks in a dolphinarium in Australia. After she was released, scientists were astonished to see (b) <u>the trick spreading among wild dolphins who had learnt it from the former captive.</u> There are (b) <u>many similar examples,</u> such as the way dolphins living off Western Australia learnt to hold sponges over their snouts to protect themselves when searching for spiny fish on the ocean floor. Such observations, along with others showing, for example, how dolphins could co-operate with military precision to round up shoals of fish to eat, have prompted questions about the (a) <u>brain structures that must underlie them.</u>

Size is only one factor. Researchers have found that (a) <u>brain size varies hugely from around 7oz for smaller cetacean species such as the Ganges River dolphin to more than 19lb for sperm whales, whose brains are the largest on the planet.</u> (a) <u>Human brains, by contrast, range from 2lb-4lb, while a chimp's brain is about 12oz.</u> (b) <u>When it comes to intelligence, however, brain size is less important than its size relative to the body.</u> What Marino and her colleagues found was that the cerebral cortex and neocortex of bottlenose dolphins were so large that (a/b) '<u>the anatomical ratios that assess cognitive capacity place it second only to the human brain</u>'. They also found that the (a/b) <u>brain cortex of dolphins such as the bottlenose had the same convoluted folds that are strongly linked with human intelligence.</u> Such folds increase the volume of the cortex and the ability of brain cells to interconnect with each other. 'Despite evolving along a different neuroanatomical trajectory to humans, (a) <u>cetacean brains have several features that are</u> (b) <u>correlated with complex intelligence,</u>' Marino said.

Exercise 2
Diagram 1
1 small cetacean species/Ganges River Dolphin, 2 12oz, 3 human, 4 2–4lb,
5 bottlenose dolphin, 6 sperm whale, 7 19lb

Diagram 2
1 three-year-old child, 2 bottlenose dolphin

Exercise 3
1 c (Dolphins have been declared the world's second most intelligent creatures after humans, with scientists suggesting they are so bright that they should be treated as '<u>non-human persons</u>'.)
2 a (The researchers argue that their work shows it is <u>morally unacceptable</u> to keep such intelligent animals in amusement parks or to kill them for food or by accident when fishing.)
3 e (Many dolphin brains are larger than our own ... said Lori Marino ... who has used magnetic resonance <u>imaging scans</u> to map the brains of dolphin species and compare them with those of primates.)
4 b (Such observations, along with others showing, for example, how dolphins could co-operate with military precision to round up shoals of fish to eat, have prompted questions about the <u>brain structures</u> that must underlie them.)
5 d (They also found that the <u>brain cortex</u> of dolphins such as the bottlenose had the same convoluted folds that are strongly linked with human intelligence.)

Exercise 4
1 contemporary women scientists (... she has been responsible for the most comprehensive study of wild chimpanzees – and become an idol of contemporary women scientists around the world. 'global recognition' = 'around the word'; 'a role model' = 'an idol')
2 as humans (Louis Leakey, the famous palaeontologist and Goodall's mentor, said of her work: 'Now we must redefine "tool", redefine "Man", or accept chimpanzees as humans.')
3 to be mothers (Leakey thought that the attributes that made a good field scientist were innate to women. Because women were pre-programmed to be mothers, he thought, they had three crucial traits: ... [three

examples are given as explanation here] – *all beliefs later echoed by Goodall.* 'Goodall believed' = 'all beliefs later echoed by Goodall'; 'natural' = 'innate'; 'main reason' refers to the fact that this is a summary of the three beliefs.

4 generations of women *(Since then Goodall and her two sisters in science, Fossey and Galdikas, have paved the way in primatology, a field that is now dominated by women. ... Goodall, Fossey and Galdikas have helped to inspire generations of women to pick up their binoculars and take to the world's fields and forests.* 'the three sisters in science' = 'Goodall and her two sisters in science'; 'have been encouraged ... by the example of' = 'have helped to inspire'; 'field scientists' = 'pick up their binoculars and take to the world's fields and forests'.

5 big players *(In most fields of scientific research, most of the big players continue to be men.* 'even today' = 'continue to be'; 'in the field of science ... do not tend to' = 'in most fields of scientific research'; 'women ... their role is limited' = 'big players ... men')

Part 3: Exam practice

1 Katla,   2 magma chamber(s)/reservoir(s),   3 dike/horizontal magma sheet,
4 mantle/semi-molten rock,   5 three/3,   6 twelve/12 miles

7   The job market

Part 1:   Vocabulary

Exercise 1
a 2,   b 4,   c 1,   d 5,   e 3,   f 6

Exercise 2
1 d,   2 a,   3 f,   4 b,   5 c,   6 e

Exercise 3
Suggested answers:
Universities are expanding opportunities to spend a year overseas, meaning that not only language students benefit from time spent in another culture. Amanda Harper, head of placements at Bath University, says going abroad offers students the chance to widen their cultural horizons and develop an international network of friends and contacts.

'One of my science students learnt to dance salsa and speak Spanish during his year in Costa Rica,' she says. 'The students mature and their confidence increases. These changes are unquantifiable in terms of marks but the time management skills, presentation skills and ability to deal with the world are vastly improved when they come back from their placements.'

As it becomes increasingly difficult to stand out in the graduate job market, a year's experience in another country could be what separates one student from others with the same results. A survey for the Confederation of British Industry found that 56 per cent of employers were not satisfied with graduates' foreign language skills and 40 per cent were dissatisfied with candidates' international cultural awareness.

Most overseas placements are taken in the third year of university, after which students return for a fourth and final year. Cassandra Popli, 22, who spent a year at California State University in Long Beach, got a job in California which she will take up after graduating from Swansea University this summer. 'I feel like I have got so much more from that year abroad than I would have if I had stayed here,' she adds.

Exercise 4
1 opportunities,   2 abroad,   3 (cultural) horizons,   4 develop,   5 confidence,   6 job

Exercise 5
1 f, 2 j, 3 g, 4 b, 5 i, 6 e, 7 d, 8 a, 9 c, 10 h, 11 k

Exercise 6
1 m, 2 h, 3 k, 4 d, 5 j, 6 l, 7 b, 8 e, 9 c, 10 o, 11 g, 12 a, 13 n, 14 f, 15 i

Exercise 7
5 Blue-collar workers usually get weekly wages. White-collar workers usually get a monthly salary.
6 Blue-collar workers may be self-employed. Examples of jobs are: construction worker, electrician, plumber. White-collar workers may also be self-employed. Examples of jobs are: lawyer, teacher, administrator.

Exercise 8
1 wages, 2 workforce, 3 retail, 4 network, 5 industry, 6 construction, 7 consultancy, 8 placement, 9 counterpart, 10 merchandising, 11 broadcasting, 12 veterinarian

---

Part 2:   Practice exercises

Exercise 1
Verbs: calculated, employ, market, maximise, offer, search, value
Nouns: business, consumer, job, management, market, offer, product, search, value
Adjectives: additional, calculated, economic, harmful
Note: Some nouns can function as an adjective, e.g. *job opportunities*.

Exercise 2
2 noun: 'little' is normally followed by an uncountable noun.
3 adjective: noun (subject) + 'be' (verb) + noun/adjective (This could also be a passive construction, but it is unlikely, because we expect the word to have a positive meaning, which would be hard to express with a verb here.)
4 noun: 'or' is a coordinating conjunction, so we would expect the same type of word before and after it.
5 adverb: We can expect a word that tells us more about the verb 'defined'.
6 past participle: In a passive construction, the verb 'be' is followed by a past participle.
7 relative pronoun: 'unemployment hangs like a cloud over America' gives more information about what happens in the 'picture'.
8 adjective: 'and' is a coordinating conjunction, so we would expect the same type of word before and after it.
Possible answers:
2 value, 3 promising, 4 statistics, 5 often/usually, 6 translated, 7 which, 8 pessimistic

Exercise 3
1 a, 2 c, 3 a, 4 c, 5 a, 6 b, 7 a, 8 c

Exercise 4
2: There are too many words in this answer. ('&' means 'and')

Exercise 5
The summary is about the legal rights and responsibilities of students who work.

Exercise 6
The relevant section of the text begins from the ninth paragraph ('But whether you are bar staff or an agency nurse, …)

Exercise 7
1 their rights,   2 older,   3 written contract,   4 permanent employees,   5 tax

Exercise 8
1 Job shop,   2 interview techniques,   3 (particular) skills,   4 Self-employment

---

Part 3:   Exam practice

1 change,   2 qualified,   3 in the world,   4 job-seekers

8   Twenty-somethings

Part 1:   Vocabulary

Exercise 1
a 5,   b 3,   c 4,   d 1,   e 6,   f 2

Exercise 2
1 c,   2 b,   3 a,   4 a

Exercise 3
1 NL,   2 N,   3 N,   4 NL,   5 N,   6 P,   7 NL,   8 N,   9 NL,   10 N,   11 N,   12 N,
13 N,   14 P,   15 NL

Exercise 4
a decrepit,   b senile,   c octogenarian,   d not long for this world,   e septuagarian,   f ancient

Exercise 5
(Model answer)
I am only twenty-four, so I am nowhere near <u>being over the hill</u>. I am not worried about getting older: my grandparents are <u>septuagenarians</u> and <u>octogenarians</u>, and although they are <u>not as young as they once were</u>, they have not gone <u>senile</u> in any way. In fact, my grandmother on my mother's side regularly beats me at chess!

Part 2:   Practice exercises

Exercise 1
Marriage is the only topic that is not mentioned.

Exercise 2
Suggested answers for a–c:
a quantity, portion, comparative amount/number, fraction, share, percentage
b jobless, out of a job, not working, out of work, looking for work, redundant
c the maximum level, the greatest rate, the highest percentage, a greater percentage than ever before
1 one in six,   2 928,000,   3 17.8 per cent

Exercise 3
The answers should have been quite easy to find if you read the text slowly or if you read it more than once. However, more important is the fact that you were practising increasing your reading speed.

Text 1
- How many times has the writer been married? Twice.
- Did the author divorce because he and his wife had very different backgrounds? No, because they had different ideas about their futures.
- True or false: the writer is saying that it is better to get married when both partners have already established their own identities. True.
- True or false: the writer suggests that his experience is evidence that getting married in your thirties is always better. False: there are exceptions.

Text 2
- True or false: the writer was surprised at her own decision to marry in her twenties. True.
- Do the writer and her husband own their own house? Yes, they have a mortgage.
- True or false: the writer found it hard to get used to living with somebody who is different to her and also to being married. True.
- True or false: the writer thinks that a successful marriage is more about finding the right person than about marrying at a certain age. True.

Exercise 4
1 ✓
2 not given (We can deduce that some do, and we may know that some do, but the statement does not mean that they often do.)
3 not given (We may think we know that relatively few people are having babies when they are under twenty-five, but perhaps there is the same number of babies now. Even if we know that the global birth rate is going down, the statement itself does not tell us that.)
4 ✓

Exercise 5
1 NOT GIVEN (As young people are their 'main customer base', McDonald's is *probably* busy after school hours. We may even know this to be true. However, the text does not give us that information.)
2 TRUE (*According to a Lancaster University study commissioned by the company, customer satisfaction was 20 per cent higher in those branches employing workers over 60.*)
3 FALSE (Only 1,000 out of 75,000 are over 60.)
4 NOT GIVEN (The text tells us that Morrisons is the fourth largest supermarket in Britain. The other three large supermarkets are the ones that are named here, but the text does not give us this information.)
5 NOT GIVEN (Morrisons are probably are doing well, because they have created 5,000 jobs and are creating 2,000 more. It seems difficult to imagine that they would do that if they were not in a financially good position. However, another explanation is possible: perhaps they would normally create many more jobs than they are doing. Moreover, the text does not tell us anything about their finances.)
6 NOT GIVEN (it is possible that this is true. However, perhaps Morrisons do not recruit anyone over 65, and perhaps they also recruit people younger than 18. The text does not tell us anything about the age of the other recruits.)
7 TRUE (The 2,000 jobs include vacancies for checkout operators.)

Part 3: Exam practice

Statement	Answer:
On average, women marry men who are older than them.	TRUE
Married couples in their forties are more likely to divorce than the others	TRUE
Women often stay at home while men go out to work.	NOT GIVEN
People in their thirties usually have not made much money yet.	FALSE
People's experiences in their previous relationships can damage their current relationships.	TRUE
People who marry in their thirties are pressured by their families to have children quickly.	NOT GIVEN

9 Community spirit

Part 1: Vocabulary

Exercise 1
1 d,   2 f,   3 e,   4 g,   5 a,   6 c (the vowel sounds in 'county' are pronounced like 'cloudy'),   7 b

Exercise 2
a 2,   b 3,   c 4,   d 1

Exercise 3
1 f,   2 c,   3 a,   4 e,   5 b,   6 d

Exercise 4
1 c,   2 b,   3 d,   4 e,   5 g,   6 f,   7 a,   8 h

Exercise 5
Suggested answers:
The Prince of Wales is backing a campaign by 250,000 volunteers to save Britain from unsightly development and clutter.

The initiative, entitled Street Pride, aims to mobilise communities into taking an active role to prevent local roads, squares and precincts being spoiled. Backed by 1,000 civic groups across the nation, the organisers say that they want to create a vibrant body of activists.

Griff Rhys Jones, the comedy actor and presenter, will act as the figurehead for the campaign, which will be supported by English Heritage, the well-known organisation that protects England's historic built environment.

There are already many local campaigns. Activists in Tonbridge, Kent, are determined to restart the high street clock to re-assert its importance as a landmark in the town and in St Albans, locals are opposing a warehouse development.

Elsewhere there are plans to provide good playgrounds and save open spaces for community recreation. A priority will be to work with schools and to inspire children from an early age to value their local streets and distinctive buildings.

Exercise 6
1 role,   2 group,   3 local,   4 open,   5 buildings,   6 campaign,   7 community/communities

Exercise 7
1 clutter,　2 civic,　3 a body,　4 activists,　5 a figurehead

Exercise 8
1 suburban,　2 charitable,　3 participation,　4 initiative (or initiation),　5 volunteer,
6 activist,　7 campaign

Exercise 9
1 charitable,　2 initiative,　3 suburban,　4 activist/campaigner, campaigner/activist

---

Part 2:　Practice exercises

Exercise 1
1 a,　2 b,　3 c,　4 b

Exercise 2
1 b,　2 c,　3 e,　4 a,　5 f,　6 d

Exercise 3

Text 1
(a) <u>As I have worked with volunteers and volunteer groups for many years</u>, I can vouch for the fact that the community spirit is flourishing. (b) <u>Every day I watch volunteers interacting</u> with their fellow human beings, and in so doing, enriching themselves in so many ways.

I work in Manchester, and my job is (c) <u>placing volunteers with hospices, old age homes, and care homes for children</u>. Our volunteers (c) <u>range in age from 17 to 70</u> and (c) <u>come from a wide range of backgrounds</u>, but they are all willing to give up their time in order to help others. They are proof, if proof is needed, that we live in a rich multicultural environment. (d) <u>Volunteering is one of the most powerful forces for good in our society.</u>

Text 2
Don't forget the power of local government when it comes to issues in your neighbourhood. (e) <u>In geometry, the shortest distance between two points is a straight line</u>. In politics, if you have a local issue, take the shortest route and go first to your local council. Some issues are far better dealt with at community level. I live in an area where (f) <u>there is lack of infrastructure, lack of amenities, and a risk of flooding</u>. There is a tendency to become quite angry if such issues are not dealt with. Keeping calm and electing the most level-headed member of the group as spokesperson will help your cause.

Another big problem is ghost estates, (g) <u>neighbourhoods with half-empty or empty buildings</u>. Residents should ask their local politicians what will happen to these developments and how they plan to make things better.

Exercise 4
1　b (The villagers, led by a small steering group, banded together to raise enough money to save it: *241 people bought £10 shares, with £3,000 coming from local donations and £25,000 from charitable schemes.*)
　　c (Minimal rent and free labour have helped rescue the services.)
2　a (*According to the Rural Shops Alliance, 600 country shops closed last year. Add the post office closure programme into the mix and thousands of neighbourhood hubs are being lost.*)
3　b (*The villagers, led by a small steering group, banded together to raise enough money to save it: 241 people bought £10 shares, with £3,000 coming from local donations and £25,000 from charitable schemes.*)

Exercise 5
1 Y, 2 Y, 3 Y, 4 Y, 5 N, 6 N

Exercise 6
1 c (This involves a paraphrase: 'rural' refers to the countryside, and the issue is pub closures.)
2 b (There were two successful protests: in Hesket Newmarket, people raised money and bought a pub; in Charlton Horethorne villagers set up a campaign and got The Kings Arms pub reopened.)
3 a (These days, it's far cheaper to buy alcohol in supermarkets to drink at home than it is to visit the local boozer. 'Boozer' is an informal word for 'pub'.)
4 c (The 'Pub is the Hub' is an organisation that encourages different groups to work together.)
5 c (the Prince of Wales)

Part 3: Exam practice

1 C (local environment: *people living on busy streets, open space … not kept clear*; behaviour: *reduces interaction with neighbours, graffiti, antisocial behaviour, kids mucking about*)
2 B (benefits: *an opportunity to find out*; asking around: *trying to meet the neighbours, talk to people in the pub or the corner shop*)
3 G (organisation: *hold a street party to boost community spirit*)
4 D (*a Neighbourhood (or Home) Watch scheme, share a desire to create a safe area*)
5 F (problems: *a bad image*; not really problems: *boost community spirit*)
6 A (aspects: *if the neighbours are friendly, …will get involved in helping to deliver public services, setting up social enterprises and tackling local issues*)

10   On the move

Part 1: Vocabulary

Exercise 1
a 8, b 3, c 6, d 1, e 4, f 7, g 5, h 2

Exercise 2
1 Medium-size cars have become less popular in recent years, so many more crashes involve a big vehicle hitting a small one.
2 The study found that the rise in sales of 4x4s and people-carriers was causing more than 20 extra deaths and serious injuries a year among people in small cars.
3 There is massive demand for bicycle lanes. A lot of people who are new to cycling think they are the only way they can be safe on the road, but what is really needed is for drivers to be trained to interact safely with cyclists, and cyclists to understand how to travel in congested traffic.
4 According to the council, a number of areas have been identified where maintenance has been poor and there are obstacles in the cycle paths. It claims to be addressing the problems.
5 He believes measures such as the ban on trucks in the city centre and the bicycle rental and bike-to-work schemes have been more effective in promoting cycling.
6 Travel is about gaining a greater understanding of other cultures: in today's survey 70% said it was important to experience cultures in other countries.
7 North America and Britain are Ireland's strongest tourist markets.

Exercise 3
1 massive public (demand),   2 congested (traffic),   3 poor (maintenance),
4 address (a problem),   5 gain (an understanding)

Exercise 4
1 b,   2 c,   3 b

Exercise 5
1 customers,   2 holiday at home,   3 business,   4 people who travel to work,
5 campaigners,   6 scheme, injuries

Exercise 6
1 collision,   2 enforcement,   3 interaction,   4 involvement,   5 congestion,   6 encounter,
7 constitution

Part 2:   Practice exercises

Exercise 1
1 F,   2 O*,   3 F
*Even if we know (after reading statement 3) that Thai Airways has won a prize for 'Best
Airport Services', that still does not mean that statement 2 is a fact. People could argue that
winning a prize is not enough, or that it depends on who voted for the prize. In other words, we
may know that a lot of people agree with the statement, but it remains an opinion.

Exercise 2
1 NO,   2 YES,   3 YES
Since then, controls on outbound travel have been relaxed <u>further</u> (Example), <u>partly</u> (2) through
the simplification of private passport and visa applications, which has <u>helped</u> (3) the demand for
independent travel, <u>particularly</u> (1) among young people.

Exercise 3
1 NO (The statement says the reasons can be put in order of importance but the text says they
   were 'split fairly evenly': the three groups were very similar in size.)
2 YES (These are all reasons: historic buildings and shopping are 'among the biggest attractions'
   and there is 'strong interest' in Premier League Football.)
3 YES (According to the text, the Chinese have 'an appetite' for luxury goods. This means they like
   them. Note how words are used in different contexts. 'Appetite' normally refers to hunger. This
   image of wanting to eat can help you understand the idea here: the Chinese have an appetite for
   certain goods, so they want to consume them, they want to have a lot of them.)
4 YES (The writer describes them as 'luxury' items, so they are not basic. 'Basic' here means the
   opposite of 'luxury'.)
5 NO (It is often said that China produces cheaper goods but the writer says that luxury goods are
   in cheaper in Britain than in China because of import taxes and tariffs.)

Exercise 4
1 league table,   2 figure,   3 rank,   4 fall,   5 rise,   6 hit,   7 predict,   8 forecast

Exercise 5
1 NG (The writer referred to 'businessmen', not to 'businesswomen'. We could therefore think that
   the writer has excluded women, and is suggesting that they do not travel for business. However,
   the writer could be using 'businessmen' to mean 'business people'. In any case, the text does not
   mention businesswomen and we cannot be sure that the writer means that Chinese women do
   not travel for business.)
2 NG (The text mentions that visiting historic buildings is a reason for travelling. We know that
   Buckingham Palace and the Tower of London are historic buildings and that many tourists visit
   them. However, the text does not mention them and we cannot use our own knowledge of the

world. This statement seems logical but you need to find out whether it is mentioned in the text and whether the writer agrees.)

3 NG (We have some information about this: we know that malt whiskies are cheaper in Britain than in China. However, the statement implies that all whiskies are cheaper, and we do not know from the text if this is true or not. Note how knowing grammar can help you work out meaning. The following three expressions have the same meaning: *Whisky is cheaper in Britain than in China. = Whiskies are cheaper in Britain than in China. = All whiskies are cheaper in Britain than in China.*)

4 YES (The text mentions the increasing ease and cheapness of travel, which means that the ease and cheapness are now greater than in the past.)

5 YES (The text says that new airports increase flight capacity, so we know that new airports have been built.)

6 YES (The text mentions the wider introduction by employers of paid leave. This means that more employers pay their employees while they are on holiday. This was given as one of the reasons why they travel more.)

Exercise 6

1

a NO (They are 'buying holidays', not staying home.)

b NOT GIVEN (We do not know why they avoid travel agents.)

c YES (One in five is the same as twenty per cent; 'travel agents' and 'travel professionals' are synonyms; 'booking directly' refers to 'avoiding travel agents' and 'booking from home')

2

a NOT GIVEN ('Being confident' has a broader meaning than 'confident about booking'. We do not know if this is the case.)

b YES (If they 'say' it, they have 'noticed' it; 'now feel more able' refers to 'becoming more confident'.)

c NOT GIVEN (We know that customers are booking more by themselves, but we do not know if that means they book more holidays than travel agents do.)

3

a YES (We know of two setbacks: customers booking by themselves and competition.)

b NOT GIVEN (We do not know what they understand about this; we just know that competition has been negative for them because they have been 'suffering' from it.)

c NO (It is getting worse: there is 'increasing pressure' for travel agents.)

4

a NOT GIVEN (We have no information about travel agents' past behaviour.)

b YES (He said they need to do things in order to 'survive'.)

c NO (He thinks they need to react more quickly: 'be faster on their feet'.)

5

a NO (He said the opposite.)

b YES ('Five years from now' means 'in five years',; 'likely' and 'probably' are similar in meaning, and if there are a third fewer, then there are two-thirds left.)

c NOT GIVEN (We know there might be fewer, but the text does not say this is because of going bankrupt; 'will' is more certain than 'will probably'.)

Part 3: Exam practice

1 NO (It is 'believed to be': it is a belief, an opinion, not a fact. The text also says that the Guinness Book of Records does not recognise it as the shortest flight, which is more evidence that it is not official.)

2 YES (The text mentions 'just over a mile' distance.)

3 NOT GIVEN (The text says the company 'offered', but it does not say that it offered to do this for free.)

4 YES (Students from 'either island' go to the capital of Orkney, Kirkwall.)
5 YES (The commercial director uses the words 'popular' and 'vital'.)
6 NO (The airline 'regularly' flies visiting subject teachers to the islands. 'Regularly' is the opposite of 'rarely'.)

11   Cultural differences

Part 1:   Vocabulary

Exercise 1
a 2, b 5, c 1, d 4, e 6, f 3

Exercise 2
Low culture: baked beans, basketball, bestsellers, bingo, electric guitars, gossip magazines, graffiti, reality television, rock concerts, romantic fiction, slapstick humour, soap operas, take-away meals
High culture: ballet, caviar, champagne, classical music, coin-collecting, horse-riding, literary festivals, novels, opera, plays by Shakespeare, poetry, polo, violins

Exercise 3
Suggested answers:
How affordable is high culture? One great myth of our time is that tickets for opera, theatre, ballet and orchestral concerts are too expensive, especially for the young. This is infuriating as, in Britain, at least, it's nonsense. The cheap tickets to hear London's orchestras range from £7 to £9 – same as a cinema ticket, and lower than at many pop and comedy venues. For comparison, when the Los Angeles Philharmonic perform with top soloists and conductors the cheapest seat is £30; and at the Berlin Philharmonic it's an expensive £46.

Finding cheap tickets to the opera and ballet isn't so easy. True, British companies don't charge the stratospheric prices found on the Continent (£2,000 for a good seat at the premiere of La Scala's *Carmen* last December), but the tickets are still pretty steep. Plump fees paid to star performers partly account for that. Luckily, however, one spectacular technological innovation has stunningly transformed the scene. It's live (or slightly delayed) cinema transmissions. The New York Metropolitan Opera now beams its shows to 800 cinemas round the world, and British companies aren't far behind. Cinematic opera is excellent value. For the cost of a good bottle of wine (£10 or £15 for the Royal Opera House's shows; £25 for the Met) you can sit in your local movie-house and see a high-definition relay of what's occurring on the world's grandest stages. No, it's not the same as being there. But in some ways it's better. The sound is impeccable. The close-ups, particularly of dancers, are enthralling. And you can react to the show as part of a live audience, rather than sitting on your own at home.

To me, this mountain of evidence, together with free museum admissions, indicates that the arts world should stop worrying that its audiences are still mostly middle-class. Anyone who can afford to visit a pub can also afford to see top-quality drama, music and dance. The real battle now should be ensuring that schoolchildren are given enough tastes of high culture to make them want to buy all those cheap tickets when they grow up.

Exercise 4
a myth,   b venue,   c conductor,   d stratospheric,   e steep,   f plump,   g stunningly,
h beam,   i relay,   j impeccable,   k enthralling

Exercise 6
1 The stratosphere is the layer of the earth's atmosphere which lies between 10 and 50 kilometres above the earth.

2 If you plump a pillow or cushion, you shake it and hit it gently so that it goes back into a rounded shape.
3 If you say that someone is beaming, you mean that they have a big smile on their face because they are happy, pleased, or proud about something.
4 If you are stunned by something, you are extremely shocked or surprised by it and are therefore unable to speak or do anything.

Exercise 7
1 a conductor,   2 a relay,   3 steep,   4 a myth

Exercise 8
(Model answer)
I come from a village where there was only one possible <u>venue</u> for cultural events. It also functioned as our village hall. Occasionally they put on films there. The nearest town had a real <u>cinema</u>, with <u>affordable tickets</u>, and my friends and I went there often. It also had a <u>museum</u> devoted to the shipbuilding industry. It was only when I moved away to attend university that I first went to a real <u>theatre</u>. I saw some <u>spectacular</u> plays and <u>stunning</u> dance performances. Now I would never want to live in a village again.

Part 2:   Practice exercises

Exercise 1
<u>Art is more important than almost anything else</u>. (opinion) <u>But it is also very difficult to do and often difficult to understand</u>. (opinion) So why should we pay for this high culture for the fun of a few? And, come to that, how should we pay? <u>Answering those questions convincingly is now more urgent than ever</u>. (opinion) <u>The government has recently announced that it will cut the arts budget</u> (fact), <u>so we need to think about what can be done</u>. (opinion)

Exercise 2
Suggested answers:
B: paediatricians' advice, children, electronic media/TV, technology, law
C: advertising, children's programmes, Britain, junk food
D: globalisation, economy, international workforce, China, cross-cultural research, job performance

Exercise 3
Suggested answers:
Paragraph 1:
Topic: cultural differences in job performance appraisal systems
traditionally: West = individual, China = collectivist principles

Paragraph 2:
Topic: aims of study: a comparison between the West and China concerning concepts of counterproductive work behaviour, task performance, and other work-related behaviour

Paragraph 3:
Topic: attitudes towards counterproductive behaviour: the West and China have similar attitudes

Paragraph 4:
Topic 1: attitudes towards task completion and individualistic aspects
Chinese managers value these more, but the West and China value cooperation equally
Topic 2: possible reasons for these results
China: now more decentralised, market-driven, competitive; industrialisation may have led to individualisation

Exercise 4

1 our research looked at two issues
2 theft from the company is unacceptable in any job
3 their scores were the same as those of bosses in the West
4 companies and their senior employees do not pay enough attention to finishing work

Exercise 5

1 C (*In Western literature, traditionally job performance appraisal systems were related to the completion of tasks specific to one's job. Chinese tradition ... is rooted in collectivist philosophies such as ... benevolence, right conduct, loyalty and good manners.*)
2 C (*stealing from the organisation, which is frowned on in any work environment, Chinese or Western*)
3 B (*But Chinese managers scored higher than Western managers on the importance placed on task completion and on individualistic aspects such as 'challenging work' and 'opportunity for advancement': 'opportunity for advancement' is a paraphrase of 'career progression' and if Chinese managers gave it a higher rating, Western managers could not have given it the highest rating. We have no information about whether Chinese managers gave it the highest rating or not.*)
4 C (*They rated equally with Western managers on aspects such as 'work with people who cooperate'.*)
5 A (*China has evolved from a centralised and planned economy to a decentralised and market-driven one in 20 years.*)

Exercise 6

1 D (*The newly rebuilt Royal Shakespeare Theatre in Stratford-upon-Avon is <u>on budget and on time</u>, a message which has been repeated often by all <u>the directors, theatre consultants, project managers and PRs</u> showing people round the new building. This is a fact. It could be proved right or wrong.*)
2 A (*But it is also deeply disappointing. This is an opinion. It cannot be proved right or wrong.*)
3 C (*... £112.8 million was raised, a third privately, two thirds from the Arts Council and the regional development agency. This is a fact. It could be proved right or wrong.*)
4 B (*Theatre, says the RSC's artistic director, Michael Boyd, is about experiences 'shared in the same space in real time' ... 'The theatre experiences we most enjoy,' he adds, 'are the ones with loads of problems but bags of character.' This is an opinion. It cannot be proved right or wrong.*)

Part 3: Exam practice

1 A (*He also mentions two languages that have no exact numbers. The most studied of these is Pirahã, which is spoken by only about 400 people. It has a word for 'about one' and a word for 'about two' and A Pirahã girl was once taken out of the village ... But after returning to the community, while she retained some Portuguese she quickly forgot how to count.*)
2 F (*Our base ten system of the digits zero to nine, which has its origins in India, is now in use all over the developed world.*)
3 D (*For example, the Waimirí have words for one to three, and then say '3+1', '3+2', '3+3', '3+3+1', '3+3+2' and '3+3+3'.*)
4 B (*Animals and babies are good at discriminating quantities above five, so one would expect that the Indians are too – even though they do not have words to express such amounts. And this is exactly what experiments ... have confirmed: when given tests that involve comparing sets of more than five dots on a screen, the Munduruku scored just as high as Westerners. ... The words for three, four and five were approximations – as if what they meant to say was 'threeish', 'fourish' and 'fiveish'.*)
5 E (*Our base ten system of the digits zero to nine, which has its origins in India, is now in use all over the developed world. It is a natural system, but for several hundred years mathematicians have questioned whether it is the wisest base for us to have.*)

6 C *(For example, one tribe, the Yupno, go as high as 34: their word for 34 is 'one dead man'. These Papuan 'body-tally' systems are unusual because almost all other systems group numbers in much smaller sets.)*

12   Practice test

Your score can only give you a rough idea of what you will achieve on the reading component of the actual IELTS test, but it should help you decide whether you are ready to take the test or whether you perhaps need to revise some of the previous units. The following table is an indication of the IELTS band you might achieve based on your score on this particular practice test:

Score out of 40	IELTS band
15+	5
19+	5.5
23+	6
27+	6.5
30+	7
33+	7.5
35+	8

You get 1 point for each correct answer. Remember that spelling and grammar are important.

READING PASSAGE 1

Questions 1–5
1 Picasso/Pablo Picasso *(Picasso is one of the most iconic names in art, yet some of his ceramics and lithographs fetched less than £1,000 each at Bonhams on Thursday.)*
2 Anthony Gross *(It can be smarter to buy really good one-offs from lesser-known artists, he adds. ... For example, the Christie's sale of art from the Lehman Brothers collection on Wednesday will include Valley with cornflowers in oil by Anthony Gross)*
3 lesser-known artist *(It can be smarter to buy really good one-offs from lesser-known artists, he adds. ... For example, the Christie's sale of art from the Lehman Brothers collection on Wednesday will include Valley with cornflowers in oil by Anthony Gross)*
4 'uncool' style *(These are affordable because their style has come to be considered 'uncool' ... For example, ... a study of three Spanish girls by John Bagnold Burgess at £4,000 to £6,000.)*
5 oil painting *(Meanwhile, the Sotheby's Impressionist and modern art sale in New York features a 1962 oil by the Vietnamese Vu Cao Dam)*

Questions 6–9
6 vii *(the biggest 'affordable' category for top artists is 'multiples' — prints such as screenprints or lithographs in limited editions)*
7 iii *('There's still prejudice against prints; these types of works are currently about as 'cheap as they can get' and will hold their value in the long run)*
8 vi *(Valley with cornflowers in oil by Anthony Gross; The sale also has oils by the popular Mary Fedden)*
9 iv *(The examples suggest that Victorian painters seemed to like real life topics, and the following are mentioned: landscapes, three Spanish girls, works depicting poverty.)*

Questions 10–13

10 TRUE (In paragraph 1, Picasso and Warhol are named as 'big-name artists'; Picasso, Matisse, Miró and Steinlen are mentioned in paragraph 3 as 'top artists'.)

11 NOT GIVEN (Ceramics and multiples (screenprints and lithographs) have sold for this amount, but paintings are not mentioned.)

12 NOT GIVEN (We may know that this is unlikely, but the text does not say anything about the price of greeting cards. It just says that oils by Mary Fedden have been sold for that amount of money, and that her works are often shown on greetings cards.)

13 FALSE (It is true that the risks are high, but the main idea in this sentence is that 'investing in new artists or markets is not worth it'. However, the passage states that it can be worthwhile: 'worthwhile only if ...'; 'A further way of making money'.)

READING PASSAGE 2

Questions 14–15

14 B (A stream of rescue vehicles, satellite television trucks and vehicles carrying journalists from around the world are heading up to the shallow bowl in this lunar landscape that will be a centre of attention over the next few days.)

15 A (If the rock walls are deemed stable the miners could be brought out, one by one, within another two or three days.)

Questions 16–20

16 freed,　17 trained,　18 reached,　19 designed,　20 estimated

Questions 21–26

21 steel
22 53cm
23 (LED) lights
24 oxygen tanks/escape hatch
25 escape hatch/oxygen tanks
26 (retractable) wheels/sets of wheels

Question 27

A (All the other headings apply to the text to some extent, but the main purpose of the text is to announce the good news that the miners are likely to be rescued soon.)

READING PASSAGE 3

Questions 28–32

28 B vi (Some evidence suggests that it is helpful... However, many claim that better lighting is just as effective... there is conflicting evidence)

29 C iii (in order for CCTV to have any effect, it must be used in a targeted way. Most schemes that simply record ... do not produce results. CCTV can also have the opposite effect of that intended. 'All the evidence suggests that CCTV alone makes no positive impact on crime reduction and prevention at all.)

30 D ii (police are considering using more technology.)

31 E i (a toy-sized remote-control craft that hovers above streets or crowds to film what's going on beneath... small enough to be unnoticed by people on the ground ...high-resolution video surveillance equipment and an infrared night vision capability... bird's-eye view of locations ... virtually undetectable)

32 F viii (<u>disadvantages</u>: ... *who will get access to this technology? In theory, this technology could be used against motorists. And where will the surveillance society end? ... if it's another weapon to be used to invade our privacy then we don't want it;* <u>advantages</u>: *looking for antisocial behaviour... crime detection ... aid rescue attempts ... monitoring of illegal fly tipping and oil spills ... As long as high-tech tools are being used in the fight against crime and terrorism, fine.)*

Note: B mentions the cost of cameras (iv), C mentions a (false) sense of safety (x), D and F mention 'cars and cameras' (vii) and E mentions 'serious crime' (v) but those are not the main points of the paragraphs.

Questions 33–35

33 B *(In Britain we've already got the world's biggest DNA database.)*
Incorrect answers:
A: It is more than 4 million, but that does not mean the same as 5 million.
C: This is not mentioned in relation to Britain.
D: This will happen next year.

34 C *(CCTV can also have the opposite effect of that intended, by giving citizens a false sense of security and encouraging them to be careless with property and personal safety.)*
Incorrect answers:
A: Manchester is mentioned but we do not know where Professor Press usually works.
B: A particular study is mentioned but he studies design and crime prevention.
D: Professor Press believes that some marketing departments (those of security companies) 'promote the crime-reducing benefits of their products'. He does not say that this is a lie but suggests that there are other ways to reduce crime.

35 D *(They contain high-resolution video surveillance equipment and an infrared night vision capability, so even in darkness they give their operators a bird's-eye view of locations while remaining virtually undetectable.)*
Incorrect answers:
A: The Microdone is not a toy, and its shape is not mentioned.
B: The Metropolitan Police do not use it (yet).
C: The government is not mentioned.

Questions 36–37

36 rock concerts, football
37 private security firms

Questions 38–40

38 NOT GIVEN (The author comments on the fact that Britain uses a lot of technology to fight crime, that technology is improving and that the police need it these days, but it does not say anything about whether the amount used is right or not.)
39 YES (The author says that it could be used against motorists in theory.)
40 YES (The last sentence in the passage says that it should not be used to invade privacy.)